Elite • 144

# US World War II Amphibious Tactics

Mediterranean & European Theaters

Gordon L Rottman • Illustrated by Peter Dennis
*Consultant editor* Martin Windrow

First published in Great Britain in 2006 by Osprey Publishing,
PO Box 883, Oxford, OX1 9PL, UK
PO Box 3985, New York, NY 10185-3985, USA
Email: info@ospreypublishing.com

Osprey Publishing is part of the Osprey Group.

© 2006 Osprey Publishing Ltd.

All rights reserved. Apart from any fair dealing for the purpose of private study, research, criticism or review, as permitted under the Copyright, Designs and Patents Act, 1988, no part of this publication may be reproduced, stored in a retrieval system, or transmitted in any form or by any means, electronic, electrical, chemical, mechanical, optical, photocopying, recording or otherwise, without the prior written permission of the copyright owner. Enquiries should be addressed to the Publishers.

Transferred to digital print on demand 2014

First published 2006
1st impression 2006

Printed and bound by PrintOnDemand-Worldwide.com, Peterborough, UK

A CIP catalogue record for this book is available from the British Library

ISBN: 978 1 84176 954 7

Editorial by Martin Windrow
Page layout by Ken Vail Graphic Design, Cambridge, UK
Index by Glyn Sutcliffe
Originated by PPS Grasmere, Leeds, UK
Typeset in Helvetica Neue and ITC New Baskerville

**The Woodland Trust**
Osprey Publishing is supporting the Woodland Trust, the UK's leading woodland conservation charity, by funding the dedication of trees.

www.ospreypublishing.com

**Author's Note**
Unless otherwise credited, all images are courtesy of the National Archives, US Navy Historical Center and the US Army Center for Military History.

**Artist's Note**
Readers may care to note that the original paintings from which the color plates in this book were prepared are available for private sale. All reproduction copyright whatsoever is retained by the Publishers. All enquiries should be addressed to:

Peter Dennis,
Fieldhead,
The Park,
Mansfield,
Notts
NG18 2AT,
UK

Email: magie.h@ntlworld.com

The Publishers regret that they can enter into no correspondence upon this matter.

**Abbreviations and ship/craft designations**

| | |
|---|---|
| ArmdDiv | Armored division |
| InfDiv | Infantry division |
| MarDiv | Marine division |
| AKA | Attack cargo ship |
| AM | Minesweeper |
| AO | Oiler/tanker |
| APA | Attack transport ship |
| BB | Battleship |
| CA | Cruiser |
| CL | Light cruiser |
| CV | Aircraft carrier |
| CVE | Escort carrier |
| CVL | Light carrier |
| DD | Destroyer |
| DE | Destroyer escort |
| LCA | Landing craft, assault |
| LCI | Landing craft, infantry |
| LCI(L) | Landing craft, infantry, large |
| LCM | Landing craft, mechanized |
| LCT | Landing craft, tank |
| LCT(A) | Landing craft, tank, armored |
| LCVP | Landing craft, vehicle or personnel |
| LSI | Landing ship, infantry |
| LST | Landing ship, tank |
| LVT | Landing vehicle, tracked – "amtrac" |
| PC | Patrol craft |
| PT | Patrol torpedo boat |
| SC | Submarine chaser |

# US WORLD WAR II AMPHIBIOUS TACTICS

## INTRODUCTION

While over 40 amphibious assaults of regimental or larger size were conducted in the Pacific Theater, the European and Mediterranean Theaters of Operation (EMTO) saw far fewer. The Pacific war was essentially a naval campaign supported by the Marine Corps, Army, and the land- and carrier-based air arms of all three services. The EMTO was a two-continent land campaign supported by the combined naval forces of the United States and the British Commonwealth.

Most of the landings were multi-division, even multi-corps in size. Rather than landing the forces necessary to secure comparatively small islands, EMTO landings had the aim of establishing large invasion forces ashore to seize lodgments and seaports from which to commence land campaigns to liberate whole continents, supported by massive land-based air forces.

Most of the landings occurred in the Mediterranean Sea, on the coasts of North Africa, Sicily, Italy and Southern France. "The Med" extends some 2,400 miles east to west, covering three time zones, with a maximum north–south width of 1,000 miles. In the 1940s it was bordered by Spain, France, Italy, Yugoslavia, Albania, Greece, Turkey, Syria, Palestine, Egypt, Libya, Tunisia, Algeria, and French and Spanish Morocco – a total of 28,600 miles of varied coastline. Passages at both ends – the Strait of Gibraltar connecting with the Atlantic Ocean in the west, and the Suez Canal connecting with the Indian Ocean via the Red Sea in the east – were controlled by the British throughout the war.

The Mediterranean is divided into two distinct areas. The eastern Mediterranean is characterized by countless small coastal islands, while the western sea possesses several large islands including Sicily, Corsica and Sardinia. From the "toe of the boot" of Italy a shallow submarine ridge stretches under Sicily and Malta towards Tunisia; this serves as the dividing line between the eastern and western Mediterranean. With the exception of two British landings on the "toe and sole" of Italy's boot, all of the major amphibious operations occurred in the western Mediterranean. The region's climate

After all the planning, gathering of intelligence, deceptions, assembly of men and materiel, theorizing and rehearsals, this was the only place where the questions could finally be answered. Landing beaches might be completely free from obstacles, but an amphibious landing force had to be prepared to overcome extensive manmade defenses, as seen in this low-level air reconnaissance photo of a Normandy beach at low tide. Construction workers can be seen scattering in fear among the antiboat ramps, stakes, tetrahedrons and "hedgehogs" – see also Plate D.

features wet but relatively mild winters and hot, dry summers. Major destructive storms are infrequent, and tidal changes insignificant. Unlike the Pacific, the Mediterranean was well charted after millennia of nautical trade. By the end of 1942 Axis naval forces posed only a minor threat, with air attack being of more concern.

The other locale for amphibious operations in the EMTO was the English Channel, the narrow seaway separating Britain from France. Here natural obstacles were few, as were significant islands, and the waters were minutely charted. Its width varies from just 20 miles at the Strait of Dover in the east, where the Channel joins the North Sea, to 110 miles separating Land's End, the westernmost tip of southern England, from Brest in Normandy, the westernmost point of France, where the Channel opens into the Atlantic. The major natural threat is brutal Atlantic windstorms blasting in from the northwest, to churn the narrow waters confined by the rockbound coasts of England and France. The coastal defenses of Germany's *Atlantikwall* posed a significant obstacle to any landing.

Most areas in the Mediterranean and European theaters where landings were executed offered good beaches with few natural obstacles, the most common being shallow sandbars running parallel to shore. A major factor affecting landings in the Pacific was absent in the EMTO – coral reefs. With the notable exceptions of Normandy and Southern France, few if any manmade obstacles were encountered. Concrete seawalls existed in some areas, but in most cases these were low and relatively easy to overcome. Beach gradients were usually gradual and shallow; since they extended well offshore this presented an obstacle to all but very shallow draft beaching vessels. This was so important that the Landing Ship, Tank and other beaching craft were even designed with the Channel's typical 1-to-60 beach gradient in mind.

The beaches are generally broad, not overly deep, and sufficiently solid to support vehicle traffic. Those in the Med are typically of hard-packed sand. Channel beaches are often covered with shingle (smooth pebbles or small rocks); this surface provides poor traction for wheeled and tracked vehicles. Frequently the natural obstacles that caused the most difficulties were the belts of sand dunes edging beaches. Heaped by wind and wave action, these low dunes of fine, soft sand made vehicle passage difficult and required bulldozed paths and some form of surfacing to support traffic. Bluffs behind beaches also posed obstacles: they usually presented shallow slopes, but gave the defenders unrestricted fields of fire, and exit routes from the beaches often ran up easily defended gullies. In most instances well-developed road networks allowed the assault force to move inland to its initial objectives.

Throughout this text, readers should bear in mind that no two amphibious operations were planned, organized or executed in exactly the same way. Available units and resources, mission, terrain, enemy forces, and evolving doctrine all dictated this variety. Lessons learned from previous operations were studied and implemented. Every operation saw the introduction of new types of units, equipment, tactics, techniques and procedures, resulting in a constantly evolving form of warfare.

# AMPHIBIOUS DOCTRINE

The US Marine Corps was the lead service in the development of amphibious assault tactics. Pre-war fleet landing exercises were of relatively small scale, and the Navy was preoccupied with the battle line and aviation. With the establishment of the Fleet Marine Force in 1933, Marine and Navy amphibious warfare development increased, but only slowly, and funding was limited. In 1934 the Marine Corps published a *Tentative Manual for Landing Operations*, and this provided the basis of amphibious doctrine for all three services.[1] The Navy adopted this manual in 1937, and as *Fleet Training Publication No.167* the following year, and this remained in effect throughout the war. Until 1943 the Army did not find it necessary to adopt it, but in that year it was issued as FM 31-5, *Landings on a Hostile Shore*. The Army was more concerned with defending the Continental United States and overseas territories. Any overseas expeditionary forces were expected to be transported by the Army's own transports and the Navy, to land at secure seaports – as during World War I; the Army had little interest in amphibious landings, considering that such matters fell within the perview of the sea services.

The Army began to take more interest in amphibious operations in 1940, and limited exercises were conducted; but it was not until 1942, shortly after the US entered World War II, that the Army began serious efforts to develop such operations and undertake large-scale training. As late as April 1942 the Army was still proposing that it should be responsible for amphibious operations in the Atlantic, and the Marines in the Pacific. The Marines were initially envisioned as operating in both oceans, and the East Coast-based 1st Marine Division was included in early plans for North Africa. However, the Marines were to fight only in the Pacific while the Army served in both theaters. Eighteen of the Army's 21 divisions in the Pacific would conduct 26 major landings; most of these were either lightly opposed or unopposed. This was far from the case in most of the EMTO landings, which were either strongly opposed at the shoreline or met heavy resistance very shortly after landing.

Between 1940 and 1942 joint training efforts often highlighted doctrinal differences between the Army and Marines. These were usually minor, and involved issues of command and control and logistics which were normally resolved during actual joint operations. However, one major difference was that the Army initially preferred night landings and the Marines daylight. In the event, night landings proved to be impractical for all but small-scale raids; they presented great difficulties of control over troops and fire, locating beaches, avoiding obstacles, locating enemy positions and other factors. Nonetheless, many of the Army landings were conducted at night, generally two hours before sunrise.

Regardless of how well organized and equipped an assault force might be, any seriously opposed amphibious assault was quickly overtaken by confusion. Landing craft were sunk, or grounded; units were landed in the wrong places, or facing more difficult terrain than expected; they might find themselves without equipment that had been central to their planned role, or left leaderless by the loss of key personnel; opposition might be heavier than anticipated, or from an unexpected direction. Only the superior training, leadership and motivation that enabled troops to improvise under fire could make the landing "stick", despite the inevitable disruption of the originally planned sequence of events.

Here wounded are treated under fire on a pebble beach in Normandy, June 6, 1944. Two men still wear the inflatable life belts issued for the landing – more a psychological encouragement than a practical aid.

---

[1] See Elite 117, *US World War II Amphibious Tactics – Army & Marine Corps, Pacific Theater.*

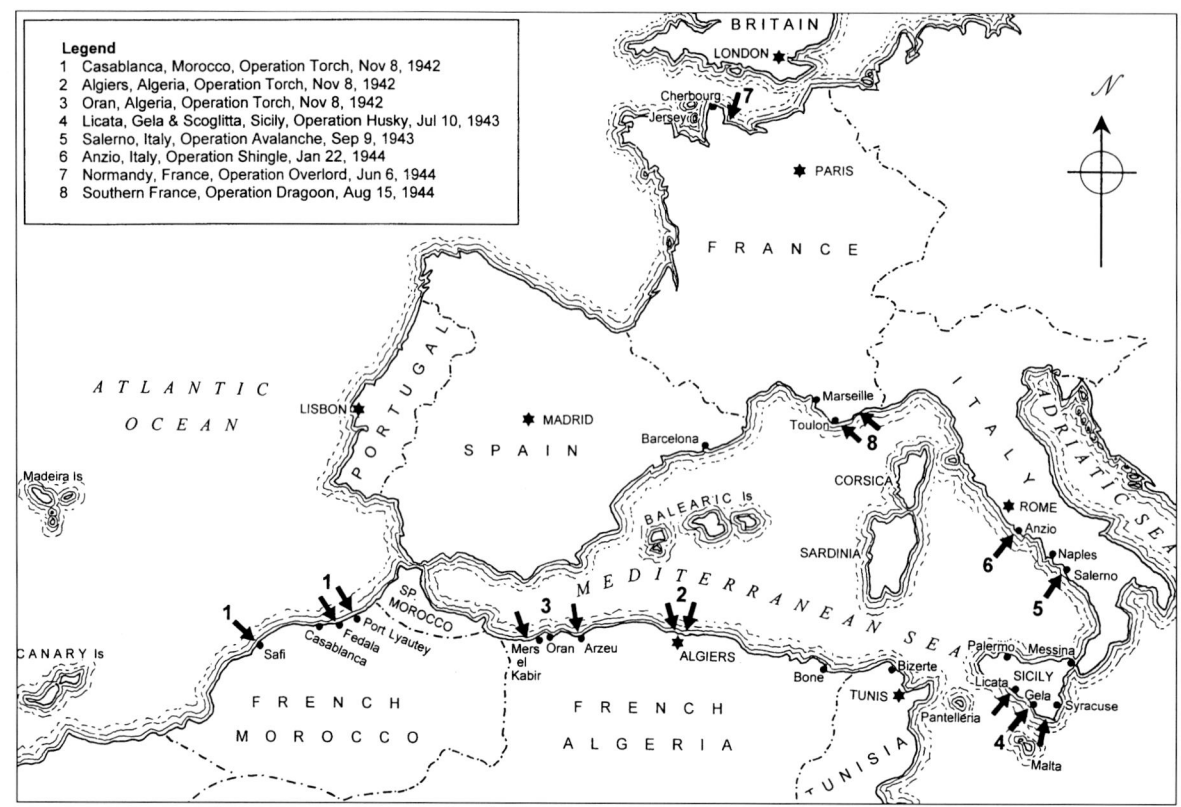

**Major amphibious operations in the EMTO, 1942–44.**

Between the World Wars there had been so few joint Army/Navy amphibious exercises, with such inconsistent participation by key commanders, that any lessons learned were forgotten and no joint doctrine was developed. When the Army first began participating in amphibious training with the Navy and Marines they were content to follow the sea services' lead; but by 1942 the Army was dissatisfied with the training, planning, and execution of such exercises. They accused the sea services of providing insufficient transport and landing craft; of failure to adequately train naval aviation to support ground troops, or to undertake sufficient practice in shore bombardment; and of often landing troops on the wrong beaches. US Navy officers also studied British Royal Navy amphibious doctrine, but this lacked a unified command concept; until the Americans had obtained operational experience it was not possible to further develop a doctrine.

### Contingency plans, 1940–41

The Army's first potential amphibious operation was the result of an unforeseen situation. In early summer 1940, French forces on the Caribbean islands of Martinique and Guadeloupe and in French Guyana declared in favor of the new pro-Nazi Vichy government. It was feared that ten French warships, including an aircraft carrier and two cruisers, might flee to North Africa and possibly fall under German control. Fearing that islands in the Caribbean might come under German control, in June the US declared that it would not recognize the transfer of Western Hemisphere territories from one European power to another. This declaration was rejected by Germany.

The Emergency Striking Force was formed in July 1940 with the mission of seizing the islands and interdicting the French fleet if it left port. This joint expeditionary force was composed of the 1st Marine Brigade at Guantanamo Bay, Cuba, and the Army's 1st Division in New York – the only available combat-ready Army division that had undertaken limited amphibious training. In the event the crisis passed, but the force was again alerted in November 1940. (In May 1942 the French ships and aircraft were finally demilitarized, and French Caribbean forces surrendered in June 1943.)

In June 1941 the Emergency Striking Force was expanded to I Corps (Provisional), Atlantic Fleet. This comprised the 1st MarDiv (former 1st Marine Bde), the Army's 1st Div (now in Virginia), and dedicated Army Air Corps and Marine Aviation elements. The Marines would have conducted the initial assault landings with the Army units following. A Panama-based parachute battalion was also assigned, and this would set a precedent: most amphibious operations in the EMTO would be supported by airborne landings, a concept entirely unforeseen earlier. I Corps was tasked with training an amphibious force for possible expeditionary landings in North Africa, on French Caribbean possessions, the Azores and Cape Verde Islands, or to reinforce Panama Canal defenses. Even though the US had not yet entered the war, a combined US/British landing plan for North Africa was developed, employing the 1st Marine and five US Army divisions. The plan was abandoned in January 1942 owing to the lack of shipping and other necessary resources. Besides contingency operations I Corps had a training mission; in August 1942 it was redesignated the Atlantic Amphibious Force, and its first large scale landing exercise was conducted.

This joint contingency and training force was not without its problems. There were disagreements between the three services over differences in organization, communications, administration, supply, objectives and customs. Service-unique radios were unable to communicate with others. There were many doctrinal differences, including the argument over daytime or night landings as already mentioned; others included the employment of air support and

A jeep disembarks from an LCV onto Sommerfield trackway across a beach (see Plate G). The early-war LCV designed by Higgins was the first ramped beaching craft adopted, but it was short-lived. The raised pulpit for the coxswain at the stern meant that such craft could not be stacked or "nested" when stowed aboard transport ships.

By 1943 beaching craft with hugely greater capacity were coming into service, such as this Landing Ship, Tank – note the 40mm and 20mm antiaircraft gun tubs above the bow. The LSTs are finished in the Measure 22 camouflage scheme widely used in the Mediterranean and the English Channel; this was a graded system, with the hull navy-blue and the sides above the deck line painted pale or "haze"-gray. The prominent identification number was repeated above the inner bow doors, for the benefit of embarking troops. The success of an amphibious assault depended upon many preparations long before the actual landing, and a key phase was the marshaling and loading of the landing force; here $\frac{1}{4}$-ton jeeps with $\frac{1}{4}$-ton trailers wait to embark.

artillery, with the artillery-poor Marines placing more reliance on naval gunfire. The concept of a joint Army/Marine amphibious force was being questioned by early 1942, due both to such doctrinal differences and to the Marine Corps' expansion difficulties.

### Separation of Army and Marine spheres of operations, 1942

In March 1942 the force was once again redesignated, as Amphibious Corps, Atlantic Fleet. By this time it had been decided to employ the Marines solely in the Pacific. The 1st MarDiv was shipped to New Zealand and Samoa, and the 2nd MarDiv followed in stages. During its entire existence the Atlantic amphibious force was commanded by a Marine general, but the Marine staff now departed for the West Coast to organize V Amphibious Corps Headquarters. In August 1942 – the month that the 1st MarDiv landed on Guadalcanal in the Solomons – the Amphibious Corps, Atlantic Fleet was transferred to the Army, with 2nd Armored, 3rd and 9th Infantry Divisions. The Amphibious Corps was never employed as such, and was disestablished in October 1942.

The pre-war concepts of amphibious operations were usually at a comparatively small scale. The small Marine Corps would provide units to conduct the initial opposed landing, with Army units to follow. Primary goals were to seize a seaport and airfield, if present, so as to allow the debarkation of large units and supplies. The airfield would be repaired and serve as a base for close air support aircraft. The developing scope of World War II would of course prove this concept inadequate for the EMTO. With the Marines now totally committed to the Pacific, it would be left to the Army to develop, organize, instruct and deploy combat and support units adequately trained in amphibious warfare. The Army also felt strongly that only they were capable of executing and sustaining major land campaigns, since the Marines were a much smaller expeditionary force lacking the necessary massive logistics and support capabilities.

Naturally, the Navy was also heavily involved in the development of amphibious doctrine, but the Joint Chiefs of Staff directed that the Army would be responsible for training; they would establish amphibious training centers to instruct selected divisions in shore-to-shore operations, while ship-to-shore training would be provided by the Navy. The two services never fully trusted one another; on the eve of the North African landings MajGen George Patton bluntly stated that "Never in history has the Navy landed an army at the planned time and place." Fortunately, while there were still problems, later amphibious assaults proved that this was not inevitably the case.

### The lessons of experience

Doctrine evolved throughout the war by the analysis and implementation of lessons learned in actual operations. Some lessons were gleaned from the Pacific, but this was not an overriding source of doctrinal change in the EMTO. While every operation saw the introduction of new tactics and techniques, it was the Sicily landings in July 1943 that taught the most lessons and prompted the most widespread changes. This was the first landing in which the new landing ships and craft were available, along with pontoon causeways. Parachute and glider units were used for the first time in support of an amphibious assault; their employment was flawed, but it was realized that they could provide valuable support.

In the context of German-occupied France, the ill-fated British/Canadian landing at Dieppe in August 1942 had already provided many lessons at a high cost in lives. This had been a test to determine if a seaport could be taken by a direct frontal amphibious assault, and to determine the effectiveness of the German defenses and response. In the aftermath of Dieppe it was understood that a mass concentration of force would be necessary in a specific area, rather than widely dispersed multiple landings along the French coast. Although the latter approach was successful in North Africa and Sicily, the circumstances in northern France would be very different. A lodgment area with a seaport was necessary, in which the landing force could build up and airfields could be refurbished or built.

Even with experience previously gained through exercises and operations, commands conducted experiments of their own to further develop and improve tactics and techniques. For example, the many problems encountered in landings on hostile shores were studied by Naval Forces, Europe, and included: waterproofing vehicles and tanks, wading trials to determine their maximum wading depth, design and trials of LCT ramp extensions, LCT beaching trials, Rhino ferry trials, trials of small landing craft in surf, testing the suitability of LSTs as hospital ships, the most efficient means of discharging stores from a coaster, methods for clearing beach obstacles, and the quickest means to re-float stranded landing craft.

A striking impression of the massive and time-consuming logistics effort inseparable from any amphibious operation. At the bottom of this picture can be seen M4 Sherman medium tanks fitted with fording stacks.

## Planning an amphibious landing

All aspects of such operations demanded extremely detailed planning at all echelons. Once Army and Navy units were designated to conduct the operation, ports of embarkation with the necessary facilities and ship capacity had to be selected. Marshaling areas for troop units, training and rehearsal areas, and sites for stockpiling masses of supplies and equipment were selected and assigned. Training, rehearsal, loading, embarkation and convoy movement plans were made, and in some instances these were more complex than the actual landing plans. The troop and naval units were task-organized and elements cross-attached for each operation. The EMTO had an advantage over the Pacific in that the relatively close seaports and staging bases made unnecessary the vast train of oilers, ammunition, replenishment and repair ships that supported the Pacific fleets.

The invasion convoys were organized into task forces, task groups, task units and task elements. The routes of convoys, and where they would take up station once they arrived off the far shore, were planned in detail, and the departure dates and times of the different elements were calculated based on the speed of their slowest ships; for example, the LST groups would have to depart first. Air cover was planned to protect the convoys en route, along with naval escorts (the main threats being torpedo boats and submarines), and the approaches, anchorage areas and boat lanes were swept for mines. For the actual assault, plans for the employment of air and naval gunfire support were developed.

Deception efforts also played their part: the enemy knew that a landing was coming, but not when or exactly where. This often underappreciated aspect of the planning sought to misdirect the enemy's attention to an alternative stretch of coastline, to mislead his timing expectations, and to deceive him into believing that more forces were committed than actually existed. Deception operations continued right up to the moment of landing, in the form of demonstration landings, "beach jumper" deception efforts, paratrooper and commando raids, air attacks and shore bombardment in other than the actual landing areas. In later operations even dummy paratroopers were dropped, and "window" (clouds of aluminum foil strips) were jettisoned from aircraft and vessels to blind enemy radar.

The allocation of landing ships and craft was critical: not only were landing craft assigned to deliver the assault waves, but they were also scheduled to return to their mother ships to embark and deliver the many subsequent waves. Landing craft from one transport might be tasked to deliver troops from other ships than their own. The inevitable losses among landing craft during the assault had to be taken into account; more were actually lost to broaching, capsizing, swamping, collisions, natural obstacles and mechanical problems than to enemy action and manmade obstacles. Detailed plans were made as to exactly how many and what types of landing craft were assigned to each wave on each beach, along with the troop units, equipment, and supplies.

In the foreground, Seabees of a Naval Construction Battalion fit the "jewelry" that fastened pontoon sections together to form causeways and ferries. Behind them a "Duck" amphibian truck passes a "Rhino" ferry, constructed from pontoons, carrying a heavy load of vehicles.

Army shore party and Navy beach party plans were highly detailed. These assigned landing sites for different categories of supplies and equipment, laid down where dumps would be established, and took into account such diverse and essential aspects as available road networks, the recovery and repair of landing craft, the siting of command and communications posts, the staging areas for subsequent landing units and vehicles, the locations for maintenance and repair sites, reserve units, artillery and antiaircraft firing positions, and much more. Beach exit routes were another important consideration.

**US EMTO Amphibious Operations**

Divisional-sized opposed landings (only initial assault units are listed, not follow-on units). Note that British and Canadian forces participated in most of these landings, either in their own sectors or alongside US forces; in such cases only US formations are listed here:

| Operation | Date | Assault Force | Codename |
|---|---|---|---|
| Casablanca, Morocco | Nov 8, 42 | 2nd Armd, 3rd & 9th (–) InfDivs | Torch |
| Oran, Algeria | Nov 8, 42 | 1st Armd (–) & 1st InfDivs | Torch |
| Algiers, Algeria | Nov 8, 42 | 34th InfDiv, elmts 1st Armd & 9th InfDivs | Torch |
| Licata, Sicily | Jul 10, 43 | 3rd InfDiv | Husky |
| Gela, Sicily | Jul 10, 43 | 1st InfDiv | Husky |
| Scoglitti, Sicily | Jul 10, 43 | 45th InfDiv | Husky |
| Salerno, Italy | Sep 9, 43 | 3rd InfDiv, 6615th Ranger Force | Avalanche |
| Anzio, Italy | Jan 22, 44 | 36th InfDiv | Shingle |
| Normandy, France | Jun 6, 44 | 1st, 4th & 29th InfDivs | Overlord |
| Southern France | Aug 16, 44 | 3rd, 36th & 45th InfDivs, 1st Spl Svc Force | Dragoon |

# AMPHIBIOUS FORCES

The Navy established several bases where Amphibious Force personnel received training in landing craft operation, maintenance and control, communications, air support and gunfire control, intelligence, and other skills. On the East Coast these included Solomons Island, MD (not to be confused with the Solomon Islands in the South Pacific); Little Creek, VA; and Fort Pierce, FL. These bases trained landing ship and craft crews, pontoon units, Seabees, and a whole range of amphibious specialists as well as conducting training and exercises for Army units.

**Navy Amphibious Forces**

The Navy's Amphibious Forces were a broad category of units and organizations that included amphibious squadrons, landing craft flotillas, naval construction battalions, naval beach battalions, naval demolition combat units, beach jumpers, advance base units, and supporting units including radar, communication and medical.

In February 1942 Amphibious Forces, Atlantic Fleet was established at Norfolk, VA. In the Mediterranean the Eighth Fleet, with 8th Amphibious Force, oversaw US Navy operations. In the British Isles and English Channel naval forces were under the Twelfth Fleet with 11th Amphibious Force (redesignated Ninth Fleet and Amphibious Forces, Europe, respectively, prior to August 1943). Twelfth Fleet doubled as US Navy Forces, Europe, itself under the Atlantic Fleet headquartered in Norfolk, VA, and also oversaw the Eighth Fleet.

Although the Coast Guard and the Army operated some landing craft, most of the crews were provided by the US Navy. They were part of the ship's company of the crafts' parent assault transport or assault cargo ship. This LCVP is manned by the coxswain – right, at the wheel; a motor machinist's mate – left; and two boat crewmen manning the .30cal machine guns in the rear tubs. Navy personnel whose duties took them onto the beach displayed light gray bands painted round their helmets, and "USN" on their helmets and/or jackets, to prevent them being press-ganged as infantry replacements.

A fleet "amphibious force" was usually under a rear admiral and could be of any size and composition. The assigned ships and craft varied greatly: new types were commissioned, ships were frequently reassigned between commands, and forces were task-organized differently for each operation.

In April 1940, LCdr Maurice E.Curtis proposed that Navy task organization designations be standardized to replace the unwieldy system of functional nomenclatures then in use (e.g., Cruiser Scouting Force, Bombardment Force, etc.). It was impossible to predict what nomenclatures would be required to support a given operation; a new communications plan had to be developed for each, making reorganizations difficult during the conduct of an exercise or operation. Curtis proposed prearranged numerical designators allowing for the easy activation and deactivation of task organizations, and the establishment of standard fleet-wide communications plans.

Task force designations included both a number and a functional designation; the latter might change between operations, but the number and consequently the pre-assigned communications plan remained unchanged. The Navy designation system used numbers beginning with that of the parent fleet, e.g., TF 80 – Western Naval Task Force was formed by the Eighth Fleet. Subordinate task components were designated by decimal point numbers, e.g., Task Group 80.1. Additional task forces would be assigned to TF 80, such as TF 81, 85, 86, and 87. Each task force and group also bore a descriptive mission title, which could change for each operation. Task forces were asymmetrical, with variable hierarchy, composition, and organization. The system allows great flexibility, with no fixed size specified for component subdivisions, from largest to smallest: task force (TF), task group (TG), task unit (TU), and task element (TE).

The task organization and hierarchy of Navy components could be quite intricate. Navy units – squadrons, flotillas, groups and divisions – were type commands comprising specific types of ships for administrative purposes; but when task-organized, these were broken up and mixes of ships from different units were assigned to TGs, TUs and TEs as required.

Landing ships and large landing craft were organized into flotillas each of three groups. The groups were numbered in sequence through the flotillas: LCI Flotilla 1 (LCIFlot 1) had LCI Groups 1, 2, and 3; LCI Flotilla 4 had LCI Groups 10, 11, and 12, and so on. Groups were divided into two divisions, which were also numbered in sequence: Divisions 1–6 were assigned to LCIFlot 1. LST and LSM flotillas usually had 12 craft, as did LCI/LSM gunboat flotillas; LCI flotillas had 24 craft and LCT flotillas 36. (The number of craft assigned to a flotilla often varied, however.)

## Naval Construction Battalions

Among the Navy organizations that proved invaluable for amphibious warfare the foremost were the Naval Construction Battalions (NCB), more popularly known as "Seabees" (from the initials CB). Before the war the USN employed contracted civilian construction firms to build overseas Pacific area bases, but with war on the horizon it was realized that such contractors could not be exposed to potential combat. (Hundreds of civilian contractors were in fact interned by the Japanese after being trapped on Wake Island.) Headquarters Construction Companies were formed in late 1941, and the formation of NCBs was approved on January 5, 1942.

Navy regulations permitted command authority to line officers only. The Naval Construction Corps was abolished in June 1940 and combined with the Engineering Corps to form the Civil Engineer Corps. In March 1942, when the 1st NCB was commissioned, the Secretary of the Navy authorized Civil Engineer Corps officers to command the new units. Seabee enlisted men were recruited from skilled construction tradesmen and given petty officer ratings, making the Seabees one of the highest-paid organizations in the US forces. Training was undertaken at the US Naval Construction Training Center at Norfolk, VA, and at several smaller camps around the country. The Marine Corps provided Seabees with tactical training at NCB Training Centers at Camps Pendleton, CA, and Lejeune, NC.

Each NCB consisted of a headquarters and four construction companies, with 1,105 personnel. They were well-equipped, self-contained units capable of virtually any field construction task, to include building advance navy operating bases, docks, airfields,

Navy Seabees were equipped and trained for combat as well as their multitude of construction tasks; although the NCBs in the EMTO never had to join the infantry battle, they often came under shellfire and air attack. These Seabees throw themselves down on a pontoon ramp as German artillery blasts the area, while an LCT(6) closes in to dock and discharge. Note the bolted steel strips holding the pontoon assembly together.

A two-lane pontoon causeway slopes up the beach onto solid ground at low tide, while a Rhino ferry approaches the T-head pier at the seaward end, and an LCM(3) approaches from the right. Rhino ferries received cargo and vehicles from LSTs and transport ships and shuttled them ashore.

seaplane bases, road networks, supply depots, troop camps, warehouses and other facilities. Seabee units accompanied expeditionary forces and landed immediately after the assault troops to clear debris, build roads, prepare off-loading sites, off-load cargo, reopen ports, reactivate railroads, and build any other facilities required. Famous for their ingenuity, they were capable of accomplishing virtually any task assigned them; Seabees were also trained and equipped to fight, but in the EMTO there proved to be no need for this capability.

By the end of 1942, 60 NCBs had been organized. NC Regiments were administrative headquarters capable of controlling 3–5 NCBs; and NC Brigades were formed to coordinate the activities of 2–4 regiments. By the war's end 286 NCBs had been raised, along with numerous specialized units including five pontoon operating battalions, and 40 NC special battalions to serve as stevedores for loading and unloading ships in overseas areas and as shore parties during assault landings. There were also 136 Construction Battalion Maintenance Units (CBMU) to serve on completed overseas naval bases. Also raised were 118 Naval Construction Battalion Detachments (NCBD), consisting of anything between 6 and 500 Seabees, for specialized functions: mobile field laboratory, pontoon causeway, tire retread and repair, harbor reclamation, spare parts control, and dredge operation. In all there were 8,000 officers and 238,000 enlisted men in the Seabees serving around the world, and more than 325,000 Seabees served during the war. Of all these units only a small number served in the EMTO, as follows:

*North Africa, Sicily, Italy, Southern France*
NCB 17, 54, 70, 120
CBMU 513, 566, 667, 578, 579, 611, 626
NCBD 1005, 1006, 1040
*Britain, Continental Europe*
NCB Regts 13, 25
NCB 10 (Spl), 28, 29, 30 (Spl), 69, 81, 97, 108, 111, 114, 146 (Petro)
CBMU 627, 628, 629, 636
NCBD 1106, 1048

The 25th NC Regiment was responsible for far shore beach operations at Normandy as TU 127.2.2, a component of TF 127 (Service Force) of the 12th Amphibious Force assigned to the Western Naval Task Force. It was assigned the 28th, 30th (Special), 69th, 81st, 108th (formerly 2nd Section, 97th NCB), 111th, 114th, and 146th NCBs and

CBMU 1006. Their missions included: 108th NCB – Assembly and operation of the artificial harbor (Mulberry A) at Omaha Beach. 81st and 111th NCBs, and CBMU 1006 – Operation of Rhino ferries, Rhino tugs, warping tugs, pontoon causeways, dry docks, and repair of Rhino barges at Utah and Omaha Beaches. 146th NCB – Construction, operation and maintenance of petroleum, oil and lubricants installations at Utah and Omaha. 81st and 111th NCBs – Construction and operation of naval beach camps at Utah and Omaha. 28th NCB – Provision of construction element to Drews (special naval base units for repairing and operating captured seaports).

## Naval Beach Battalions

Not employed in the Pacific, these provided the core of the Navy beach party organization in the EMTO. Beach battalions, under the control of a Navy beachmaster, directed the arrival and flow of troops and supplies on landing beaches. They were not Seabees, but specialists trained for their functions at naval amphibious bases. The 450-man battalions were organized into three companies, each with three self-contained platoons. Each platoon had command, communications, hydrographic, demolition, boat repair, and medical sections. Most of these jobs are self-explanatory except the hydrographic, which marked boat lanes. Of the 12 battalions, those not committed to combat were employed to load troops and supplies aboard ships at ports of embarkation.

*Navy Beach Battalion assault participation*
1st – Casablanca, Sicily, Salerno, Anzio, Southern France
2nd – Sicily, Normandy
3rd – not committed to combat
4th – Sicily, Salerno, Southern France
5th, 6th & 7th – Normandy
8th – Southern France
9th, 10th, 11th & 12th – not committed to combat

## Naval Combat Demolition Units

NCDUs began to be raised in June 1943 and were trained at the Scouts and Raiders School at Fort Pierce, FL. Members of the six-man teams came from the Seabees, Bomb Disposal School and Mine Disposal School. They were trained to destroy beach obstacles, and were usually employed to augment other Navy and Army shore units. (The Underwater Demolition Teams – UDT – used in the Pacific to reconnoiter beaches and destroy obstacles were hardly employed in the EMTO – see page 58.)

NCDUs sometimes operated Apex demolition boats; these were radio-controlled LVPs bearing 1,000lb of explosives, which were to be directed to large underwater obstacles and detonated. They were rather

Both beach and shore parties cleared obstacles and mines. Here a soldier of an Army Engineer Special Brigade – identified by the arc painted on his helmet – readies an SCR-625 mine detector before entering a minefield marked with a black-on-white German warning sign. Numerous former French mines have already been lifted and stacked, left.

Once the beachhead had been secured up to its initial inland limit it quickly became a crowded hive of activity. In the background, a road grader of an ESB unit struggles to maintain the churned surface of a beach exit lane, followed by a jeep with trailer and a DUKW ("Duck").

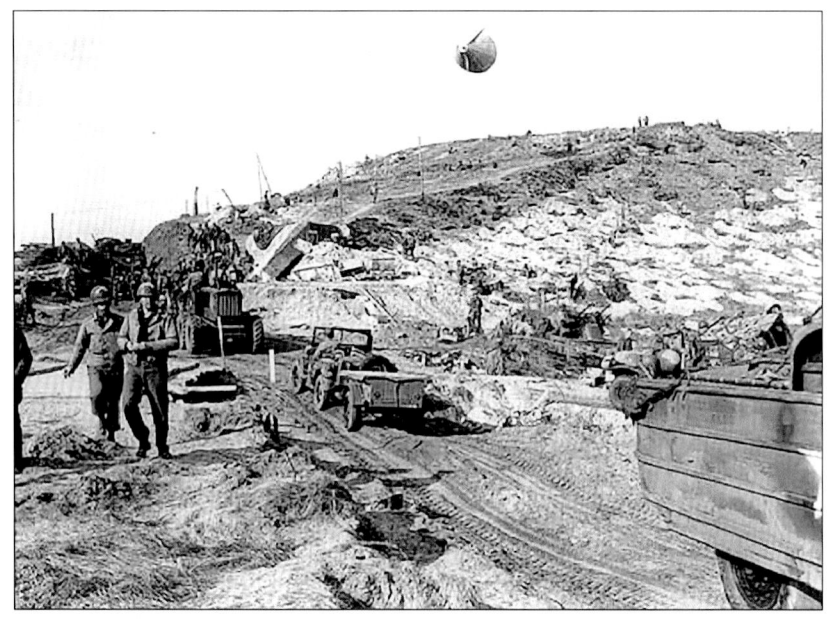

unreliable, and might wander about on their own. Another device was the Ready Fox, a large floating bangalore torpedo that was towed among obstacles, anchored and detonated.

**Beach Jumpers**

The British had developed elaborate deception techniques to mislead the enemy as to when and where landings would occur. In late 1942 US Navy Lt Douglas Fairbanks, Jr, served as an exchange officer with the Royal Navy, participating in commando raids; impressed by the deception methods, he proposed that the USN form a unit to conduct similar operations. In March 1943 volunteers reported to the Amphibious Training Base at Camp Bradford, VA. Beach Jumper Unit 1 was commissioned with the basic mission of assisting and supporting operating forces in the conduct of tactical cover and deception in naval warfare. The 480-man unit was equipped with ten 63ft air-sea rescue (ASR) boats fitted with ten 3.5in rocket launchers for radar-reflective "window", smoke generators, smoke pots, floating time-delay explosive packs, tape recorders with loudspeakers and radio jammers. They could also tow barrage balloons dangling window strips.

The concept was for the unit's boats to approach shore in a likely landing area under cover of darkness, to lay smoke screens, fire machine guns and flares, detonate explosive charges, and broadcast recordings of anchor chains dropping, boats being lowered and ship's loudspeaker announcements; they would also provide false radar reflections. These efforts to simulate a landing force naturally took place many miles from the actual landing beaches. They might be augmented by other craft conducting landing demonstrations, as well as by air activity, and by a few ships off the coast. The first operation they supported was the Sicily landing. Additional units were raised; Beach Jumper Units 1, 3, 4 & 5 operated in the Mediterranean, but none served in the Channel. (There are several theories as to the origin of the units' designation, the most plausible being simply that it was a deceptively imprecise title.)

## Army Engineer Amphibian Command

The Navy was unable to provide sufficient landing craft crews to support the projected large-scale amphibious operations worldwide. It was even forced to employ Coast Guard crews to man 76 LSTs, 28 LCI(L)s and numerous smaller landing craft. (The Coast Guard was transferred from the Treasury Department to the Navy Department between November 1941 and January 1946.) The Army organized the Engineer Amphibian Command (EAC) at Camp Edwards, MA, in June 1942 in an effort to alleviate the shortfall; in October the Center relocated to Camp Gordon Johnson at Carrabelle, FL. A conflict soon arose between the Army and Navy over the responsibility for training boat crews and the control of landing craft units. It was eventually decided that the EAC would support shore-to-shore amphibious operations as opposed to ship-to-shore, the Navy's prerogative.

The 1st–4th Engineer Amphibian Brigades were activated in the States in 1942–43, and in May 1943 they were redesignated Engineer Special Brigades. Only the 1st ESB was to serve in the EMTO: in North Africa (but not in any landings), and in the assaults on Sicily, Salerno and Normandy, where it operated as the Utah Beach Command. The provisional 5th and 6th ESBs were formed in Britain from engineer combat groups to support Omaha Beach operations under the Provisional ESB Group, as the Omaha Beach Command.

Each 7,400-man ESB usually possessed two engineer boat and shore regiments viewed as "specialized" supply and transport units. Regiments had an unnumbered boat battalion and a shore battalion capable of providing an infantry division with all necessary landing craft in the form of 650 LCMs, LCVPs and other small craft, as well as shore party support. In the EMTO only the 1st ESB operated in this manner, and it was later reduced mainly to providing shore party support, as were the 5th and 6th ESBs. For the Normandy landings they were task-organized with scores of specialist detachments from many units, and bore no similarity to the original configuration. The 1st ESB at Utah Beach was formed of no fewer than 90 small units and detachments, among which were seven amphibious truck companies, 25 quartermaster companies of various types, and 16 transportation port companies. The Provisional ESB Group at Omaha Beach with the 5th and 6th ESBs included 110 units and detachments.

These did not operate as originally envisioned, providing shore-to-shore landing craft and shore party duties; a July 1942 agreement between the Army and Navy had made the latter service responsible for all landing vessel operations in the European Theater. The ESB served as stevedores on the near and far shores, and provided shore parties and auxiliary far shore engineer services. Only the 591st Engineer Boat Regt operated as originally envisioned, at Oran in North Africa.

---

**1st Engineer Special Brigade, Utah Beach, Normandy**

Attached regimental- and battalion-sized units:

HQ and HQ Company, 1st ESB
38th Engineer General Service Regt
   1st & 2nd Bns
531st Engineer Shore Regt
   1st, 2nd & 3rd Shore Bns
2nd Naval Beach Bn
24th Transportation Amphibious Truck Bn
191st Ordnance Bn
261st Medical Bn
244th, 262nd, 306th, 537th & 577th Quartermaster Bns
490th, 518th & 519th Quartermaster Port Bns

**Provisional Engineer Special Brigade Group, Omaha Beach, Normandy**

Attached regimental- and battalion-sized units:

HQ and HQ Company, Prov ESB Group
2nd Bn, 358th General Service Regt

**5th Engineer Special Brigade**
HQ and HQ Company, 5th ESB
6th Naval Beach Bn
61st Medical Bn
251st Ordnance Bn
37th, 336th & 348th Engineer Construction Bns
131st, 533rd & 619th Quartermaster Bns
487th & 502nd Quartermaster Port Bns

**6th Engineer Special Brigade**
HQ and HQ Company, 6th ESB
7th Naval Beach Bn
60th Medical Bn
74th Ordnance Bn
147th, 149th & 203rd Engineer Construction Bns
95th, 538th & 280th Quartermaster Bns
494th & 517th Quartermaster Port Bns

**11th Port**
HQ and HQ Company, 11th Port
512th Quartermaster Group
509th, 514th & 516th Quartermaster Port Bns
174th, 512th, 554th, 688th & 4058th Quartermaster Bns

*Note:* Other than Port Bns, Quartermaster battalions were either Service or Mobile.

# LANDING FORCES

Eight US Army infantry and two armored divisions participated in amphibious assaults in the EMTO (those conducting multiple assaults are parenthesized): the 1st (2), 3rd (3), 4th, 9th, 29th, 34th, 36th (2) and 45th (2) InfDivs, and the 1st and 2nd Armored Divisions.

**Infantry divisions** were not specifically organized to conduct amphibious assaults, but they were task-organized, augmented with specialized units, and given specialized training. They were also provided with some specialized equipment, and some of their heavy equipment and vehicles might be left behind to rejoin later. Upgrading certain divisions as amphibious assault formations was considered for Normandy, but this was rejected: once they had penetrated the coastal defenses they would have to be reconstituted as standard infantry.

Army infantry division structure remained fairly constant throughout the war with only minor strength changes. An infantry division had three infantry regiments, each with three infantry battalions plus cannon (75mm halftrack-mounted or 105mm towed), antitank (37mm or, after mid-1943, 57mm) and service companies, and a medical detachment. Division artillery had one 155mm and three 105mm howitzer field artillery battalions. Combat engineer and medical battalions, plus signal, ordnance light maintenance and quartermaster companies, and a company-size reconnaissance troop, completed the division. It was common for a tank and/or tank destroyer battalion to be attached, along with an antiaircraft artillery automatic (AAA) weapon battalion with 40mm guns and .50cal quad machine guns. A chemical battalion (motorized) with 4.2in mortars might be attached. An additional combat engineer battalion, transportation truck companies, medical units, and numerous small service support units might also be attached. A standard 14,000-man infantry division could be reinforced up to 22,000 troops with these attachments. The following example is representative:

*1st Infantry Division (Reinforced),*
*Omaha Beach, Normandy*
HQ Company, 1st Infantry Division
16th Regimental Combat Team (RCT)
18th RCT
26th RCT
1st Infantry Division Artillery
5th Field Artillery (FA) Bn (155mm)
7th FA Bn (105mm)
32nd FA Bn (105mm)
33rd FA Bn (105mm)
1st Engineer Combat Battalion

**Troops descend ladders into landing craft; their lack of packs identifies this as a simple ship-to-shore movement rather than an exercise in assault landing. These ladders are made of chain with wooden rungs; more common were simple rope "landing nets". Soldiers were taught to grip the verticals, to avoid the man above stepping on their hands.**

1st Medical Battalion
1st Cavalry Reconnaissance Troop, Mechanized
1st Signal Co
1st Quartermaster Co
701st Ordnance Light Maintenance Co
Military Police Platoon, 1st Infantry Division
1st Counter Intelligence Corps Detachment

*29th Infantry Division attachments*
115th RCT
116th RCT
Provisional Ranger Force (2nd & 5th Ranger Bns)
111th FA Bn (105mm)
detachment, 29th Recon Trp, Mech
detachment, 121st Engineer Combat Bn

*Non-divisional attachments*
58th Armored FA Bn (105mm)
299th Engineer Combat Bn
635th Tank Destroyer Bn (self-propelled – M10)
741st Tank Bn
745th Tank Bn
81st Chemical Bn (Mot) ( – Cos B & C)
Co A, 56th Signal Bn

**Armored divisions** were of two types, light and heavy. The 1st and 2nd ArmdDivs when they landed in North Africa were of the heavy type (only the 2nd and 3rd ArmdDivs remained heavy throughout the war). The 14,600-man heavy division consisted of two brigade-level combat commands (A and B), with two three-battalion armored regiments (390 tanks total). There was an armored infantry regiment with three halftrack-mounted battalions. Division artillery consisted of three 105mm self-propelled howitzer battalions. Divisional units included armored reconnaissance, armored engineer combat, ordnance, quartermaster and medical battalions, and a signal company. Tank destroyer and AAA battalions were often attached.

The 10,800-man light armored divisions, reorganized in late 1943 from heavy divisions, had basically the same support units. The combat units now consisted of three battalions each of tanks (310 tanks total), armored infantry and self-propelled field artillery, under three combat commands (A, B, and Reserve). Any mix of battalions could be attached to a combat command, as well as additional augmenting battalions.

A similar scene, from above: an assault section/boat team clambering down into an LCVP. They carry only light combat packs; note, ahead of the coxswain at the right stern, long engineer pole charges – see also Plate B.

Infantry regiments were task-organized into **regimental combat teams**, exact organization varying greatly depending on the mission, situation, and available supporting units. After the North Africa landings it was recommended that RCTs for an amphibious landing would include field artillery, AAA and engineer shore battalions, engineer combat and medical collecting companies, and a signal detachment. A company of light or medium tanks or tank destroyers might also be attached. Later the artillery battalions usually remained under division artillery control, but one was normally placed in direct support of each RCT (though they could fire in support of any other regiment.)

RCTs could be tailored and augmented as required. The following example, a 29th InfDiv RCT attached to the 1st InfDiv for the assault on Omaha Beach, Normandy on June 6, 1944, is much more heavily augmented than the usual RCT, especially in regards to engineer units. This is not only because – like all other RCTs at Normandy – it was conducting an amphibious assault, but also because it was on the extreme right (west) flank of the landing. Note among its detachments elements of the 6th ESB:

*116th Regimental Combat Team, Omaha Beach, Normandy*
Main HQ, 116th Infantry
Alternate HQ, 116th Inf
1st Bn, 116th Inf
2nd Bn, 116th Inf
3rd Bn, 116th Inf
Antitank Co, 116th Inf
Cannon Co, 116th Inf
Medical Detachment, 116th Inf
5th Ranger Infantry Bn
Cos A, B & C, 2nd Ranger Infantry Bn
58th Armored FA Bn (105mm)
104th Medical Bn
111th FA Bn (105mm)
112th Engineer Combat Bn
121st Engineer Combat Bn
146th Engineer Combat Bn (organized
    into 4 combat teams)
149th Engineer Combat Bn (beach unit)
467th AAA Weapons Bn
743rd Tank Bn
Co B, 81st Chemical Bn (Mot)
461st Transportation Amphibious Truck Co
detachment, 6th Engineer Special Bde
detachment, 29th Signal Bn

Infantry battalions were similarly task-organized as **battalion landing teams** (BLT). The various units attached to RCTs were not always broken down and attached to BLTs; most were kept under RCT control, and elements could be attached to battalions as needed. A BLT might include an AT gun platoon from regiment, and maybe

*The boat team have loaded and an LCVP is ready to get underway. Astern of it, another landing craft has its bow ramp shutter open to allow the coxswain forward vision; it is closed on the ramp in the foreground. These soldiers may have long, wet hours to endure before they make their run to shore.*

A 105mm M7B1 self-propelled howitzer wades ashore. This was the standard equipment for the artillery battalions of armored divisions; it was also fielded by separate battalions that were sometimes attached to infantry divisions, and used as assault guns in support of their regimental combat teams.

an engineer platoon (often organized into gapping teams with demolitions); tank and AAA platoons were sometimes attached, plus shore and beach communication teams, shore fire control parties and air liaison parties. Organization varied greatly; only an RCT's two assault battalions might be organized and augmented as BLTs, with the reserve battalion retaining standard organization. At Normandy a typical BLT consisted of an infantry battalion, a 105mm howitzer battalion, a company of DD ("swimming") Sherman tanks, two engineer combat companies, a medical detachment and a beach party:

*Typical battalion landing team, Normandy*
Battalion HQ & HQ company
Three rifle companies
Heavy weapons company
Medical detachment
Tank company ( – one platoon)
Chemical mortar company (–) or platoon
Engineer combat platoon (one or two)
Forward observer party
Naval gunfire control party

The first waves ashore were, of course, infantry assault troops augmented with demolition and obstacle-clearing troops. The assault troops were well armed but only with light weapons; it was recognized that they might have to wade or swim ashore, negotiate beach obstacles, move quickly across exposed beaches, fight their way through defensive positions and fight off counterattacks. Heavier weapons, artillery, antitank guns and more armor would be landed in later waves, when the beach was secure and lanes had been cleared through obstacles and minefields to allow them to advance inland. (They would not have been able to do much good bunched up on the beach under artillery fire and air attack.)

An assault section from the 2nd Ranger Bn loaded into the protected bay of a British LCA at Weymouth, England, before crossing the Channel for their assault on Pointe-du-Hoc on June 6, 1944. A BAR man can be seen at left, and a bazooka man at right.

### Boat teams

For landings, rifle companies were organized into boat teams. Since the assault landing craft – LCP(R), LVP, LCA and LCVP – carried 30-plus personnel, and rifle platoons numbered 41 troops plus attached personnel, it was impossible for them all to ride in one craft, and unrealistic to expect them to be able to consolidate at once if landed from multiple craft. Instead they were organized into self-sufficient boat teams (also known as assault sections), and would fight as such until platoons and companies were able to consolidate during a lull or after securing their first inland objective.

A 199-man rifle company was conventionally organized into a headquarters; three rifle platoons, each with a headquarters and three 12-man rifle squads (each with a Browning Automatic Rifle); and a weapons platoon, with a machine gun section (2x .30cal MGs) and a mortar section (3x 60mm mortars). Assault units were almost always at least at full strength, sometimes augmented with extra troops to allow for the inevitable casualties.

For landing the company was organized into six boat teams/assault sections, subdivided into specialized teams of riflemen, BAR men, wire cutters, demolition men, 60mm mortar men, bazooka men and flamethrower operators (see Plate B for details). A seventh landing craft carried the company command group and attached personnel; these latter included artillery forward observers, medics, gapping teams, and guides and liaison personnel for later landing units. The battalion heavy weapons company had two machine gun platoons (4x .30cal M1917A1 HMGs) and a mortar platoon (6x 81mm mortars).

Usually a battalion's first wave went in with two rifle companies, to be followed by the weapons company and then the reserve rifle company and battalion headquarters; a small assault command post might accompany the lead assault companies. The reserve company would also be organized into boat teams in case it had to be substituted for one of the lead companies, or heavy resistance was still encountered upon landing. Subsequent waves would land antitank guns, tanks, engineers, medical and signal elements, regimental reserve battalions, artillery and AAA weapons. Regimental reserve battalions usually retained their standard organization so that they could fight as cohesive units immediately upon landing.

**Ranger battalions** played an important role in most landings. Modeled on the British Commandos, the Ranger battalions were essentially amphibious raiders, and their light infantry hit-and-run role once ashore was secondary. They were employed to neutralize gun positions or seize remote key terrain features on the flanks of the main landings. Their assault participation was as follows:

| Battalion | Operation |
|---|---|
| 1st Ranger Bn | North Africa |
| 1st, 3rd & 4th Ranger Bns | Sicily, Salerno, Anzio |
| 2nd & 5th Ranger Bns | Normandy |

**Airborne troops** provided another capability valuable for supporting amphibious landings.[2] Parachute and glider units were inserted in darkness before the morning amphibious landing. Their missions varied, but usually involved seizing key terrain features (bridges, causeways, road intersections, dominating hills, etc.) to aid the inland advance of the amphibious forces. They also ambushed and harassed enemy units advancing to reinforce the beach defenders or to counterattack. Since they were often widely scattered, airborne troops would also attack targets of opportunity, such as dispersed enemy elements, artillery and AA positions, command posts, logistics facilities and convoys.

**Corps troops** were augmented extensively with engineer, antiaircraft, signal, transport, ordnance, quartermaster and medical units. Once the lodgment was secured and the build-up commenced the excess units would be transferred to follow-on corps and divisions. Amphibious-specific units would assist with the build-up and logistic efforts or be withdrawn for use elsewhere; some were assigned normal engineer and transport tasks to augment those types of units.

The Army 2½-ton DUKW-53 amphibian truck was invaluable for ferrying supplies and equipment ashore and delivering them to inland dumps. They were frequently used for delivering 105mm howitzers and keeping them supplied with ammunition. Here British-manned "Ducks" line up beside a cargo ship to receive sling loads of 105mm ammunition during one of the joint Allied landings in the Mediterranean.

## Specialized training

Much attention was given to the training of landing forces. In 1943 in preparation for Normandy the USN established eight major amphibious training centers and numerous smaller bases in Britain for training crews and maintaining landing vessels. The Army established the Assault Training Center at Woolacombe, Devonshire, on the southwest coast. Some 2,000 personnel manned the base and another 2,700 served as support and demonstration troops, including the 156th Infantry; almost 800 Navy personnel provided landing craft support. Training from individual to regimental levels was conducted there, with landings on

---

[2] See Elite 136, *World War II Airborne Warfare Tactics*, and Battle Orders 22, *US Airborne Units in the Mediterranean Theater 1942–44*

Crewmen of an M4A3 Sherman medium tank already fitted with the MT-3 fording adaption install the exhaust stack of the MT-S fording kit; the intake stack is already in place ahead of it. The accompanying T-O waterproofing kit included sealing compound and tape, paint, brushes and welding rods – it took hours to prepare vehicles for wading. Once prepared, their operation was compromised; turrets could not be rotated nor guns elevated without breaking the seals. When they reached shore it took up to an hour to remove everything, although built-in detonating cord could be fired at the flick of a switch to blow off some of the seals, and quick-release cables allowed the stacks to be jettisoned. See also Plate F.

the broad beach at Woolacombe Sands. There was an artillery range, plus training areas for demolitions and amphibious trucks. Large-scale exercises and rehearsals were also conducted at Slapton Sands.

**Specialized equipment**

"Amtracs" – landing vehicles, tracked (LVT) – were deployed in huge numbers in the Pacific but saw only limited use in the EMTO. They were originally envisioned as cargo vehicles able to ferry supplies from ships across reefs and beaches. During the November 1943 Tarawa Atoll assault amtracs were found ideal for delivering assault troops across reefs that landing craft were unable to cross, while providing a degree of protection. From that point an assault division was provided with up to 400 amtracs and amphibian tanks to land the assault waves.

It is often questioned why amtracs were not similarly used in the EMTO, and there are several reasons. Firstly, insufficient numbers were available, and the priority went to the Pacific, where there was an unavoidable necessity of crossing broad fringing reefs that frustrated conventional landing craft. In the Mediterranean and the Channel, landing craft could run up to and beach on the water's edge. Secondly, Japanese-held Pacific islands were often more heavily defended at the water's edge than the beaches faced in the Mediterranean. The overriding factor, however, was that surf conditions in the Mediterranean and Channel were often too rough for the low freeboard of the amtracs, while most Pacific landings were conducted within the relatively calm water of atoll lagoons or on the protected lee side of islands.

Amtracs did see some employment in the EMTO, however. Three LVT(1)s were sent for testing during the North Africa landings, but the developmental vehicles suffered mechanical difficulties. While LVT(2) Water Buffalos were not used for amphibious assaults, small numbers were used for crossing flooded areas in the Netherlands and Belgium and for crossing the Rhine and other rivers. A very small number were employed at Normandy as support vehicles, operated by amphibious truck units. No Army amphibious tractor battalions operated in Europe except those raised after VJ-Day.

Colleville, Normandy, D+1: an M4A1 still fitted with fording adapters, although the stacks themselves have been jettisoned. This Sherman is A-13, "Adeline II", of Co A, 741st Tank Bn from 1st Armd Div, which supported the infantry of the 16th RCT, 1st InfDiv on Omaha Beach on the morning of June 6. It is seen here being towed by a M31B2 (T2) recovery vehicle after taking a 50mm AT gun hit in the suspension.

The M29 and M29C Weasel cargo carriers were employed from 1943 as auxiliary support vehicles; for an amphibious mode the M29 could be converted in the field to the M29C (for Conversion). These small vehicles were mainly used to transport ammunition and supplies to forward units over difficult terrain, and were not amphibious assault vehicles. (The British sometimes used them to carry heavy items – e.g. radios – in assault landings, as in Operation "Infatuate" at Walcheren in November 1944.)

An extremely valuable vehicle was the DUKW-353, simply known as the "Duck".[3] Introduced in 1943, this amphibious 2½-ton cargo truck proved invaluable for hauling crew-served weapons, ammunition and supplies ashore, over the beach, and delivering them where needed. Afloat it could make 6mph and ashore 50–55mph. A transportation amphibious truck company had two platoons each with 24 Ducks, plus two in the company headquarters. Their first use was during the July 1943 Sicily landings.

Fording kits were available to allow tanks, recovery vehicles, halftracks, armored cars, self-propelled artillery and artillery tractors to wade ashore through several feet of water or to cross shallow rivers. These kits included materials for sealing small openings and seams. Trucks, from jeeps up to 10-ton cargo carriers, were also provided with fording kits, which included air intake and exhaust pipe extension tubing.

M4 Sherman medium and M5 Stuart light tanks were provided with dual fording stacks for the North African and subsequent landings. These allowed them to wade through almost turret-top deep water, so long as the surf was light. For Normandy a new method was introduced in the form of the duplex-drive (DD) amphibious M4 tank, discussed in the commentary to Plate E.

**Obstacle clearance doctrines**

There has been controversy over the American "failure" to employ specialized tanks for breaching obstacles, like the British. "Hobart's Funnies" of the British 79th ArmdDiv included Sherman Crab tanks

---

[3] DUKW was the General Motors Corporation's model designation: D = year model (1942), U = amphibian, K = all-wheel drive, W = dual rear axles.

Despite the fording kit, wading ashore was always hazardous for tanks, which could easily run into unseen obstacles or treacherous surfaces. This Sherman of Co C, 70th Tank Bn ran into a flooded shellhole on Utah Beach while driving in from an LCT beached below the tide line.

mounting rotating chain flails to detonate mines, Churchill Crocodile flamethrower tanks, Churchill Armored Vehicles Royal Engineers (AVRE) mounting 290mm demolition guns, and Churchills fitted to lay down canvas trackways, steel bridges and fascines to cross seawalls and antitank ditches. US Army policy was to limit the formation of overly specialized units unless absolutely necessary. Rather than forming special units, regular units were equipped and trained for the mission, or augmented with additional specialized equipment which was dumped once the mission was accomplished so that they could return to their normal equipment and role. At Normandy the US and British Commonwealth forces deployed their specialized vehicles and gapping units differently, based on their conclusions reached through experiments and demonstrations.

This all serves to demonstrate that there was no one firm doctrine. The First US Army specified that:
* Under Army command, NCDUs supplemented by combat engineers, with hand-emplaced charges, would be responsible for demolition of seaward obstacles.
* Divisional engineers would clear lanes though minefields, assault emplacements, and breach walls for their own assault echelons from the high water mark inland.
* DD tanks would be the primary source of close fire support for beach assault.

However, the Seventh US Army specified that:
* NCDUs supplemented by Army engineers would be responsible for removal of underwater obstacles.
* Primary demolition of beach obstacles would rest with shore engineer teams.
* Initial beach minefield lanes would be cleared, and beach walls blown, by tank-dozer teams.
* Initial close support fire would be provided by tanks landed from LCMs and artillery delivered by DUKWs; DD tanks would be available to task force commanders desiring them, to supplement artillery lifted by LCMs.
* Tank-mounted rocket launchers would be utilized for assault on emplacements.

Meanwhile, the British forces specified that:
* Removal of underwater obstacles would be by Naval Landing Craft Obstacle Clearance Units (1 officer + 9 seamen), assisted by Royal Engineers.
* Removal of beach obstacles would be by RE field companies using hand-emplaced charges, assisted by naval personnel.
* Specialized tank teams (i.e. from 79th ArmdDiv) would be used to pass obstacles beyond the high water mark – flails to clear lanes through minefields, tank-mounted or tank-towed bulk charges to breach seawalls, and AVRE tanks for the assault of emplacements by engineer troops, utilizing flamethrowers and bulk explosives carried inside the tanks.
* DD tanks and the guns of the 79th ArmDiv specialized tanks would support the initial infantry assault.

The demolition of underwater and beach obstacles was critical. These included a wide variety of underwater obstacles intended to impede or destroy landing craft approaching beaches. Since most landings occurred at high tide to provide for narrower beaches, obstacles were emplaced from just below the high tide line outward to at least the low tide line. Steel girder, pipe and rail obstacles of various forms were used, along with others made from logs, sawn timbers, concrete and rock; they might be fitted with mines at the top. Natural obstacles such as rock outcroppings, shallows, shoals, sandbars and wrecks were incorporated into the obstacle plan.

Beach obstacles were designed to halt and hamper the movement of armored vehicles and troops once ashore. Barbed wire obstacles, antitank ditches and walls, antitank and anti-personnel mines were common. Pre-war seawalls presented an obstacle to getting vehicles off the beach, and once they had achieved this, broken terrain behind the beach might still impede them: sand dunes, steep headland bluffs, rocks, dense vegetation, ravines, streams, rivers, canals, marshes and intentionally flooded areas.

The Navy was responsible for breaching and removing underwater obstacles to the water's edge – the high tide line; the Army breached obstacles and created gaps beyond the high tide line. Sometimes joint gapping teams of Army and Navy personnel were organized, and took care of all obstacles up to the dune line.

Loading out, LSTs finished in Measure 22 camouflage embark their cargo. LST-1020 and others in the background have 3x15 pontoon causeways fixed to their hull sides; these were cut loose as the LST approached shore, and momentum carried the sections to the beach. From release to the first vehicle driving across the causeway took less than 10 minutes. Army-operated VLA (very low altitude) barrage balloons were often tethered to LSTs as protection from strafing fighters, which were a real danger in the Italian operations. At Normandy they were cut away after the beachhead was secure: there was no significant low-altitude Luftwaffe opposition, and they posed a hazard to the many Allied aircraft over the beaches.

## Beach and shore parties

Shore party support was essential and manpower requirements immense. Across-the-beach logistics is a unique and often the most difficult component of amphibious warfare; it was also the least developed early in the war, and its evolution was continuous. The shore party concept was especially important and was fully integrated, with both Navy and Army elements.

ABOVE **Endless stacks of 105mm howitzer "cloverleaf" crates are dumped in the open along a beach; at Normandy the lack of air opposition made camouflage unnecessary, but this was not the case in Italy. The "cloverleaf" held three rounds, and needed slightly less shipping space than conventional box crates.**

RIGHT **A hastily constructed bunker protects this Navy beach party communication command post; a ship-type blinker light is set up beside a bullhorn used to give orders on the noisy, crowded beach. Stacked on the left are spare M1 tetrytol satchel charges left over from blowing up obstacles. The sailor at far left has an SCR-536 "handy-talky" radio. Note the light gray stripes painted round the Navy helmets.**

The arrival of supplies and equipment on landing beaches quickly led to congestion and confusion, as supplies piled high and units competed for scarce space in the developing beachhead. With the large scale of EMTO landing operations and the large number of follow-on troops coming ashore for weeks and even months afterwards, it was essential that seaports quickly be secured, repaired, and returned to operation. Besides Seabees and naval base operating units, the Army provided quartermaster port units backed by various engineer and transportation units to restore and operate harbors. Other units found to be under-utilized – such as chemical decontamination companies – were pressed into supplying unloading details.

Initially, there were two organizations involved in the logistical effort, respectively below and above the dune line. The "beach party" was a Navy organization under the beachmaster, and responsible for beach reconnaissance, marking beaches and navigation hazards, removing obstacles, selecting dump and bivouac sites, supervising the unloading of troops and supplies, constructing landing facilities (beach ramps, causeways), sorting and storing supplies in dumps, controlling beach traffic and landing boats, and casualty and prisoner evacuation. The "shore party" was an Army organization under the control of the landing force commander. The shore party commander was responsible for the selection and marking of routes inland, assignment of bivouac areas and dumps, movement of units and supplies from the beach to the front, and

The shore fire control elements of Navy beach parties were attached to assault divisions to coordinate naval gunfire support from bombardment groups. At Omaha Beach the bombardment group included ten destroyers, of which one was the USS *Thompson* (DD-627), seen here refueling from the USS *Arkansas* (BB-60) in May 1944. On June 6 the destroyers came dangerously close inshore to help the pinned-down infantry of the first assault wave by engaging German gun positions. Some of them provided fire support from less than 1,000 yards out, in just three fathoms (18ft) of water.

control of stragglers and prisoners. The structure of each organization was not specified; it was task-organized from available assets as the mission required.

A major flaw in pre-war landing exercises was the independent operation of Navy and Army parties, leading to predictable problems of communications, coordination and delineation of responsibilities. In August 1941, MajGen Holland Smith of the Marine Corps recommended that the two organizations be consolidated in the "shore party", this being responsible to the landing force commander (since its mission was to support troops ashore). Dedicated work details were to be established in order to prevent diminishing the landing force's fighting strength. The Navy beachmaster was designated an assistant to the Marine/Army shore party commander. The concept was approved on 1 August 1942, just in time for implementation in the Guadalcanal landing and the later landings in North Africa.

Manpower to unload landing craft was essential. The Army originally envisioned using shore battalions of ESB boat and shore regiments, but few were available in the EMTO. Several other types of units provided manpower as stevedores and for other shore duties; these included combat engineer battalions and Transportation Corps port battalions and companies, which were essentially stevedores – as were Seabee special battalions. Occasionally reserve infantry units were employed to unload vessels, but they were more often rushed into the front line as the beachhead expanded. The pre-war rule of thumb specified 100 men to unload each cargo ship discharging on the beach; experience led to higher numbers – 150 men to unload cargo ships, transports and LSTs, 50 per LCT, and 25 per LCI.

## Communications

One of the most valuable units to support amphibious assaults ashore was the joint assault signal company (JASCO). These units were an outgrowth of the "signal company, special," the air liaison parties and naval shore fire control parties. These elements were combined in early

1944 into JASCOs consisting of Army, Navy and Army Air Forces personnel. A 406-man JASCO comprised a headquarters (49 men), air liaison party (47), naval shore fire control party (38), three beach communications sections (54 each) and a signal platoon (100 men). At Normandy one was attached to each of the three ESBs (286th JASCO to 1st ESB, 293rd JASCO to 5th ESB, 294th JASCO to 6th ESB). They did not operate as complete units, since the shore fire control and air liaison sections were detached to assault divisions (prior to the JASCOs, provisional air liaison and naval shore fire control parties supported assault divisions). JASCOs coordinated and controlled naval gunfire and close air support, and operated the ESB's beach control communications system.

## LANDING SHIPS AND LANDING CRAFT

The EMTO had to compete with the Pacific Theater for amphibious warfare ships and landing craft; although the "Germany first" policy was in effect, much of the production of these vessels was sent to the far side of the world. This was unavoidably necessary because of the Pacific's long distances, the numbers of troops and amounts of cargo that had to be shipped, and the effort needed to sustain committed forces in undeveloped areas.

Attack troop transports and attack cargo ships were employed in the EMTO, but not to the same extent as in the Pacific. Given the shorter distances involved, in many cases even small landing craft could transit from bases to landing beaches. This eliminated the considerable time necessary to embark troops and materiel aboard transports, and also to disembark the landing craft and discharge troops and supplies into them.

Most early attack transports and cargo ships were converted from merchant vessels, but dedicated designs were soon being built based on Victory Class and C3 cargo ships. The different classes of these ships varied greatly in design and capacity. Transports (APA) and cargo ships (AKA) designated "attack" were defined as such because they carried a

The Harris Class attack transport USS *Hunter Liggett* (APA-14); the first "A" was habitually deleted from hull numbers, and the small white marking just visible level with the forward deckhouse is "PA-14". These APAs carried 22 LCVPs and 4 LCM(3)s, with up to 1,900 troops.

Besides carrying tanks, artillery and other vehicles, LCTs could transport large numbers of troops. This LCT(5) appears to be painted in a light blue and navy-blue camouflage scheme, perhaps a legacy of its temporary use by the British. It was launched as LCT-8, transferred to the Royal Navy and redesignated LCT-2008, then returned to the US Navy, when it was fitted with armor plate and redesignated LCT-2008(A). It lost its bow ramp on June 6 at Normandy, but remained operational.

large complement of landing craft and could unload their cargo into them over the sides while at sea; these classifications were established in February 1943. They also possessed significant antiaircraft armament. Conventional troop transports (AP), some of which were modified ocean liners, and cargo ships (AK), basically modified merchant ships, lacked landing craft and were employed to move personnel, vehicles, equipment and supplies on the lines of communication.

**Attack transport ships (APA)** usually carried more than 1,000 troops and had cargo capacity varying from less than 1,000 up to 5,500 tons. As an example, one of the most widely used was the Haskell Class built on a Victory Class hull. These 455ft ships could carry 1,561 troops plus the crew of 536, along with 2,900 tons of cargo; the embarked landing craft included 22 LCVPs, one LCP(L), one LCP(R) and two LCM(3)s. They were armed with one 5in gun, 12x 40mm in one quad and four twin mounts, and 10x 20mm cannon.

**Attack cargo ships (AKA)** had a large cargo capacity, but could carry some troops – mostly vehicle or artillery crews, so they could land with their equipment. The 459ft Andromeda Class carried 4,500 tons along with 16 LCVPs and eight LCM(3)s.

In 1943 specially designed **amphibious command ships** (AGC) appeared, converted from different types of vessel though mostly using C2 cargo ship hulls. These provided additional space for a joint operations room, war command room, flag plot, combat information center, fighter control room, voice (radio) filter room, intelligence office, photo interpretation room, map reproduction room and print shop. Additional radios and radar were also provided. The USS *Mount McKinley* (AGC-7) had a crew of 622 and space for 441 headquarters personnel. Such ships carried anywhere from 5 to 14 small landing craft of different types.

**Landing ships (LS-)** were comparatively long-range ocean-going vessels capable of delivering large numbers of vehicles, supplies and troops directly on to beaches. Their shallow draft and slow speed limited their sea-going capabilities, however. **Landing craft (LC-)** had to be transported by and launched from transport ships; they were characterized by very shallow draught, open cargo bays, and bow ramps. Both landing ships and craft were heavily armed for air defense and to provide fire support, but were lightly armored or unarmored to reduce their draft. In July 1942 a standardization agreement between the US and the UK on landing craft/ship designations resulting in existing US craft being redesignated; the gaps in mark numbers of US craft resulted from the missing numbers being applied to British designs.

Landing ship and craft construction was a massive undertaking; only prototypes were available in late 1942, and it was not until mid-1943 that the new craft began to appear in the Mediterranean in any numbers. More than 66,000 US landing ships and craft of all types were eventually constructed. (For the basic data on major types, see the commentary to Plate A.)

\* \* \*

Until 1940 the US Navy possessed no effective landing craft or other amphibious warfare ships other than a few troop transports. Previously ship's launches and lifeboats had been employed, and these proved entirely unsatisfactory. Additionally, there were no craft available for landing tanks, artillery and other vehicles other than totally inadequate barges and lighters. In the 1930s the Navy and Marine Corps experimented with various craft, all of which proved inadequate and even hazardous. It was not until 1939 that Andrew Higgins of Higgins Industries Inc in New Orleans offered a shallow draft boat designed for beaching, the "Eureka" boat. The Navy was irritated that Higgins' designs were preferred over its own poorly designed offerings, but finally conceded and adopted the Eureka in 1941 as the **Landing Craft, Personnel – LCP**. This was a 31ft boat with a blunt, rampless bow, capable of carrying 18 troops. Previously ship's davits were limited to 30ft craft and 5 tons weight; the new transports the Navy was building could accept heavier 36ft craft. From September 1941 the LCP was replaced by the similar **LCP(L)** – "L" for "large" – a 36ft boat carrying 36 troops.

*(continued on page 41)*

The Normandy landings saw the first use of larger landing craft converted to fire rockets in the inshore fire support role. These LCT(R)(3)s carried 1,094x 5in barrage rockets; fixed at an angle of 45 degrees, they had a range of 3,500 yards, but no predictable accuracy. At Omaha nine LCT(R)s bombarded the beach before the initial landings, but results from the unaimed fire were extremely disappointing.

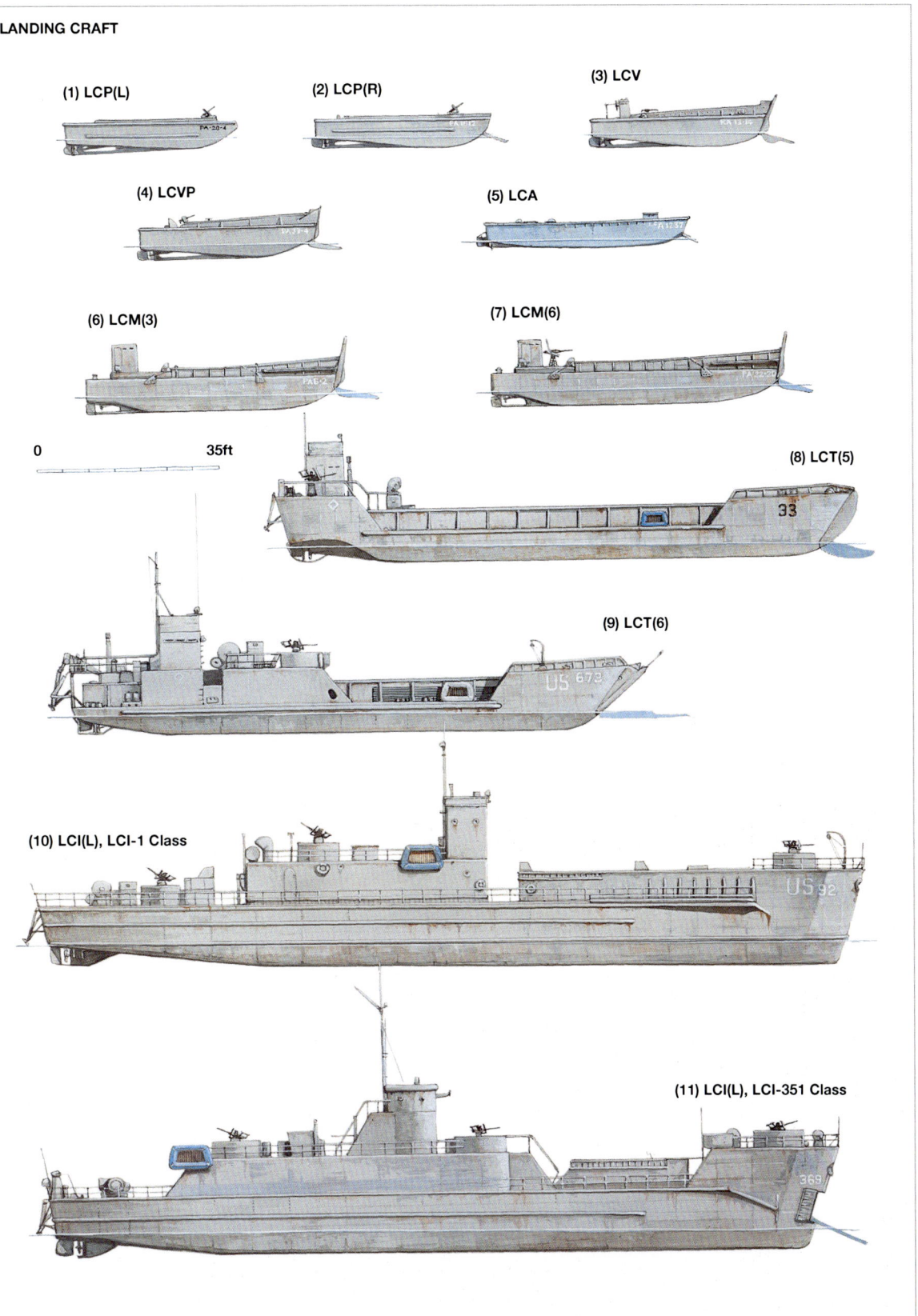

**ASSAULT BOAT TEAM**

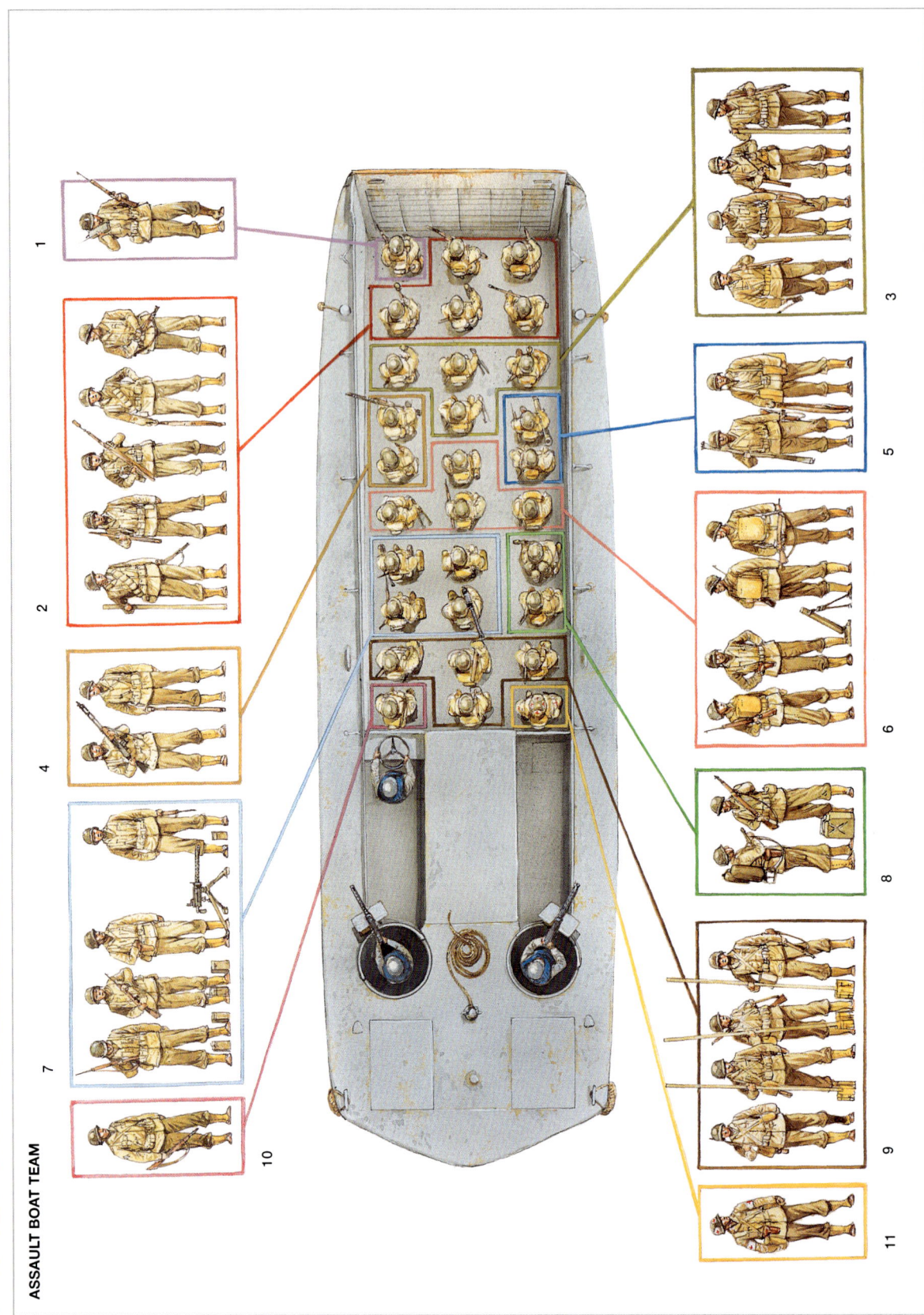

LANDING CRAFT, INFANTRY (LARGE)

C

**M4A1 SHERMAN DUPLEX-DRIVE TANK**

E

LCM AND SHERMAN TANK RIGGED FOR FORDING

CROSS-THE-BEACH TRACKWAYS

**THE ASSAULT WAVES**

In early 1941 the Marines showed Higgins a photo of a Japanese landing barge with a bow ramp; more advanced than any contemporary design, this was the *Daisatsu* (49ft, 100–120 troops), developed in the late 1920s. The Navy initially opposed the idea, since production had begun on the LCP(L) and they could not foresee that additional craft would be necessary. Bureau of Ships (BuShips) modified the LCP(L) by adding a narrow gangway through the bow and a small ramp to create the **Landing Craft, Personnel (Ramp) – LCP(R)**. However, the small ramp could not accommodate light vehicles or wheeled weapons; and at the same time Higgins designed a new ramped craft capable of carrying a jeep or 1-ton truck, antitank gun, or similar-sized equipment. This was the **Landing Craft, Vehicle – LCV**. It was soon replaced by the new **Landing Craft, Vehicle or Personnel – LCVP**. The LCVP also replaced the LCP(L), although this was retained for special purposes e.g. as a control boat. The LCVP became the most produced landing craft of the war; it was heavier than the LCV and had less cargo capacity, but it offered numerous improvements and its design allowed it to be nested (stacked) aboard transports. Owing to LCVP shortages, the British-made and manned **Landing Craft, Assault – LCA** was often used the land US troops; it had roughly the same capabilities as an LCP(R), but was fairly well armored.

Larger landing craft were necessary to deliver tanks, artillery, other vehicles and bulk cargo. Numerous designs were tested, and two were finally selected in 1942: the BuShips' **Landing Craft, Mechanized – LCM(2)**, for light tanks, and the larger Higgins **LCM(3)** for medium tanks. These were also used as utility craft. The **LCM(3)** was the largest landing craft that could be carried in davits; aboard transports an LCVP could be nested inside an LCM. The LCM(2) soon fell from use; and in 1943 the LCM(3) was supplemented by the **LCM(6)**, which was an LCM(3) with an extra 6ft midships section added to the hull. It was normally carried aboard a Landing Ship, Dock, or an LST, with smaller landing craft nested inside. Most attack transports could carry six or eight LCMs.

Still larger landing craft were needed to land multiple tanks in follow-on waves. The BuShips-designed **Landing Craft, Tank Mk V – LCT(5)** was adopted in late 1942. The 1943 **LCT(6)** was the largest US landing craft built during the war. It and the LCT(5) could be carried aboard an LST and launched broadside over the ship's side by flooding ballast tanks on one side to list the ship. An LCM could be carried inside the LCT and an LCVP inside the LCM. The LCT(5) and (6) could also be transported on a larger ship in three sections and assembled in the water; an LST could carry five such sections.

An even larger beaching vessel for tanks was needed, and the response was the **Landing Ship, Tank Mk II – LST(2)**. The LST(1) design was built by the British, but it proved unsatisfactory and they requested the Americans to redesign the vessel; the first LST(2) was

View to stern from an LCT(6) which has just left an LST after embarking a load of jeeps and trailers. The LCT(6) had a removable stern plate; it has been removed from this craft, to allow the vehicles to be driven aboard when the LCT backed up to an LST's bow ramp. The removable plate also allowed LCT(6)s to be lined up bow to stern between an LST and the beach, so vehicles could be driven off over the resultant "causeway" of LCTs.

**Heavily loaded troops prepare to embark on LCM(3)s. For the Normandy landings most LCMs made the Channel crossing under their own power rather than aboard transports. These are clearly support troops, since they are armed with M1903 bolt-action rifles instead of the semi-automatic M1 Garands of the infantry. At upper right note the rolled trackways of wooden palings and burlap – see also Plate G.**

commissioned in December 1942.[4] In order to make the flat-bottomed LST a sea-going vessel, water was pumped into the ballast tanks so that the ship would ride deeper, and pumped out as it approached shore. The LST was intended to deliver up to 30 tanks, which were carried inside in the tank deck; lighter vehicles were loaded on the weather (topside) deck. LST-1 through 512 were fitted with an elevator between the weather and tank decks; ships from LST-513 on (except LST-531) were fitted with an internal ramp instead, which proved faster for transferring deck cargo below for discharge through the bow doors. The LSTs' first operational use in the EMTO was during the July 1943 Sicily invasion. Besides carrying tanks they took all types of vehicles, heavy weapons and bulk cargo, and even served as troop transports; they could carry Ducks, which debarked at sea through the bow. Some were modified to transport pontoon sections to provide a causeway ramp extension to the beach, over twice the LST's length. Improvements were made during the LST's production to include increased armament, rearrangement of deck obstructions to allow an LCT or more vehicles to be carried, and raised conn stations to provide vision over deck-carried LCTs. Prior to Sicily, 72 LSTs were fitted with six pairs of davits and extra landing craft, since assault transports with LCVPs were not available.

Originally conceived by the British to transport Commandos across the Channel, the **Landing Craft, Infantry (Large) – LCI(L)** was developed in 1942 to land company-strength units in follow-on waves. Instead of a conventional bow ramp, this had two narrow troop gangways fitted to the hull sides. The LCI was designed to carry only troops, and no cargo or vehicles. The early class LCIs had square bridges; the improved later class, beginning with LCI-351 in May 1943, had round "castle" bridges and enlarged deckhouses, and could carry a few more troops. Most LCIs completed after May 1944, beginning with LCI-641, had the side gangways deleted and bow doors and a ramp fitted, which allowed them to carry cargo or a couple of jeeps.

---

[4] See New Vanguard 115, *Landing Ship, Tank*

The Navy developed pontoons at the Advance Base Proving Ground at Davisville, RI; here various pontoon craft can be seen, including (left foreground) a floating dry dock. By 1944 there were 31 standard pontoon assemblies, including barges (3x7, 3x12, 4x7, 4x12, 5x12, 6x18 and 10x30 pontoons); causeways (3x15, 2x30); causeway blisters (4x12); finger piers, seaplane ramps, service piers, floating small craft dry docks (7x30), fuel tank barges, and 75-ton floating cranes; self-propelled "Rhino" ferries (6x30); Rhino, warping and causeway tugs (3x7); repair barges (6x40), net tenders, and PT boat service platforms. Pontoon ferries and barges powered by outboard motors could be used as cargo and vehicle lighters, and landing craft refueling barges anchored offshore; cranes, drilling rigs and other heavy equipment could also be mounted on them.

Another British craft serving US forces was the **Landing Ship, Infantry (Medium)** and **(Small) – LSI(M)/(S)**. These were similar to US destroyer-transports and were converted from minesweepers and other vessels. They usually carried eight LCAs and 250–350+ troops, and often transported Rangers and other small units.

Large numbers of LSMs and LCIs were converted during their building to the fire support role by the addition of various combinations of machine guns, 20mm and 40mm automatic cannon, 3in and 5in guns, and banks of 4.5in and 5in rocket launchers. These included the **LSM (Rocket) – LSM(R)**, the **LCI (Gun)** and **(Rocket) – LCI(G)/(R)**, and the **LCT (Rocket) – LCT(R)**. The armament combinations varied widely; for example, the LCI(G) was found with eight different battery configurations, and some gun-armed LCI(G)s also had rockets. These larger fire support craft were not used in any numbers until Normandy; only small numbers of RN fire support craft saw use in the Mediterranean, and did not participate in every operation there. The **Landing Craft, Support (Large) – LCS(L)** was a purpose-built gunboat based on the LCI. **Landing Craft Support (Small) – LCS(S)** were converted LCP(L)s mounting machine guns and sometimes rockets, intended for inshore fire support.

When planning the 1943 Sicily landings it was discovered that shallow sandbars parallel to the beach would prevent LSTs from reaching the water's edge; consequently, the **pontoon causeway** was developed to bridge the gap. The Bureau of Yards and Docks had developed pontoons in 1939 to provide uniform-sized buoyant rectangular boxes, which could be assembled into various floating structures. The standard pontoon (P1) measured 5x5x7ft and weighed 1 ton; an unloaded pontoon drew only 16in of water, and could support a 10-ton load. Other components were a sloped bow pontoon (P2) and two-section wedge-shaped ramp pontoons (P3 and P4). These pontoons were fastened together with fittings that the Seabees called "jewelry", and long steel strips were bolted to pontoon strings to hold assemblies together. A large gasoline outboard motor mounted on the stern was provided for propelling pontoon ferries.

**LST-357 off-loads a 2½-ton truck onto a pontoon causeway. Pontoons were shipped overseas disassembled and were assembled at rear bases. Causeways up to a mile long could be created in favorable sea conditions; these were invaluable for amphibious operations, allowing LSTs and other large craft to disembark vehicles from deep water.**

Often in the Mediterranean insufficient pontoons were available, and LCT(5)s were modified by cutting out and hinging a side section. The LST would lower its ramp and the LCT would dock against it at right angles. A tank would drive into the docked LCT, another LCT would drop its ramp onto the docked LCT's lowered ramp, and the tank could turn 90 degrees to drive on to it and be carried ashore. It was a slow process, but necessary if there were a shortage of causeways; the removable stern plate of the later LCT(6) was fitted for the same purpose.

Control craft were necessary to marshal, provide navigation, and control landing craft as they assembled and made their approach to the beach, and to coordinate post-landing supply and troop delivery, casualty evacuation and many other activities. Submarine chasers (SC), patrol boats (PC), and smaller landing craft were employed in this role. Dedicated craft were built as well, including the **Landing Craft, Control Mk I – LCC(1)**. This was a 56ft boat fitted with communications, navigation, and hydrographic gear; it was crewed by 14 men and armed with three twin .50cal machine guns. The later LCC(2) had a narrower beam and was crewed by nine men and armed with two .50cal guns.

## COMMAND, CONTROL AND ORGANIZATION

At the upper echelons – theater and army group levels, where combined planning was required between US and British forces – there were broad conflicts between doctrine, command practices, staff procedures and traditions. The US employed a unified command arrangement. Even though the US armed forces did not possess a joint warfare doctrine, they realized that successful operations had to be under the command of a single commander, with authority to make and approve all decisions and with control of all units and resources, including those of other services. At lower levels – field army and fleet and lower – specific arrangements had to be worked out and coordinated. Joint planning was complex: the Army, Navy, and Army Air Forces (the latter for all practical purposes a separate service, developing its own doctrine) had their own capabilities, limitations and needs.

The British too lacked an effective joint doctrine, and they failed to establish unified commands until forced to do so by the growing complexity of the war. Instead they maintained separate staffs for each of the three services, and conducted planning and coordination by committee; plans and problem areas were, in effect, negotiated. An example of national differences can be seen in operation orders. American operation orders used a standard format, and routine and repetitive actions were specified in standard operating procedures. Short, to-the-point missions were assigned, with the mission's objective specified. As much intelligence information as was available was provided. The mission explained what to do, and when, but not how: that was left up to the subordinate commanders. These would use their judgment, experience and resources to accomplish the mission as they saw fit, while keeping within the bounds of the plan. Higher commands would provide resources and reinforcing units as required by the lower echelons to allow them to accomplish their mission. This led to fast-paced operations requiring flexibility and initiative.

The British issued complicated, detailed orders with no firm format. It was necessary for the lower echelon units to provide the higher command with information on their capabilities and what they faced. Routine procedures were specified in detail by higher headquarters. This caused delays, frequent revisions, and a less than solid plan across the board.

**After loading the assault troops, landing craft would form up and circle in designated areas until the order was given to head for the line of departure. Here, on D-Day at Normandy, LCVPs begin the move to shore under the eyes of the Western Task Force flagship USS *Augusta* (CA-31). Note the choppy sea, with waves 3ft–4ft high; the troops faced a 12-mile run, and were provided with seasickness pills (which had inconvenient side effects) and two vomit bags each. Most of the assault troops suffered horribly from seasickness during the run ashore.**

## Offshore areas

The control measures and organization of amphibious assaults differed widely as doctrine evolved and lessons were learned. They were only lightly addressed in doctrinal publications and evolved throughout the war, being tailored for each operation.

The Navy designated various seaward areas for ships supporting the landing; these would be swept by early-arriving minesweepers. "Transport areas" were between several thousands of yards and 5 miles offshore, out of most coastal artillery range but close enough to minimize the transit time for landing craft. This conserved fuel, allowing them to make more runs before refueling was necessary, and limited the troops' exposure to seasickness and enemy fire. The transport areas – one central, or one per designated beach – were large enough to disperse the ships for air attack protection. Space was also needed for landing craft to form up in waves; they would turn in large circles as loaded boats arrived from the mother ships and awaited the order to "land the landing force." A line of departure for the assault landing craft

**OMAHA BEACH AND BEACH MAINTENANCE AREA**

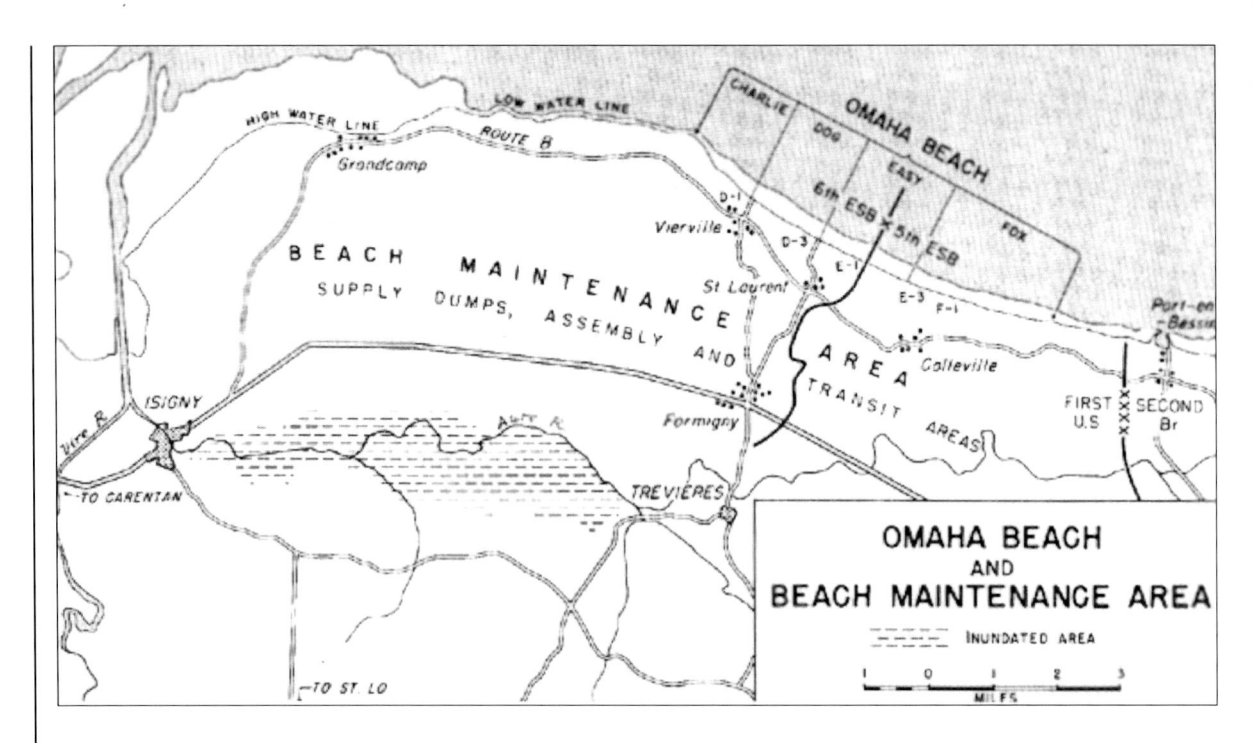

*This diagram of the Omaha beachhead at Normandy shows the extent of the ground necessary to accommodate supply dumps, assembly and transit areas, command posts, field hospitals, reserve units, artillery and AA positions – on this map, at least 9 square miles.*

was designated usually somewhere between a couple of thousand yards and 2 miles offshore (although at Normandy the first wave troops embarked 25,000 yards – nearly 12 miles – off shore). Designated boat lanes ran to the landing beaches.

"LST areas" were closer to shore, where they awaited orders to run in once the assault troops had secured the beachhead; it was here, too, that they launched and received Ducks. Other holding areas were designated for LCIs and LCTs. Start lines might be designated for the larger landing craft.

Numbered "fire support areas" were assigned for battleships, cruisers and destroyers, usually on the flanks of the transport areas. Battleships and cruisers might be positioned further to seaward of the transports, over which they fired. Inshore areas and lanes were designated for the various fire support craft. Specific areas were designated for each special task group, such as the salvage group area. "Night retirement areas" might be assigned for transports and fire support ships further out to sea, to provide maneuver space to avoid attack and collision. A destroyer screen and patrol craft would be established around the area occupied by the attack force to intercept submarines, fast attack craft and air attacks.

### Landing beaches

The beaches were designated by colors and numbers or phonetic letters and colors; the system used in the EMTO was less standardized than that used in the Pacific, and evolved over time. During the North Africa landing the pre-war system was used, in which two or more adjacent beaches were designated e.g. Red and Red 2; to prevent confusion all beaches designated by the same color were later numbered from "1" up. However, at Sicily some number 2 beaches were added to the flank and were not adjacent to the primary beach of the same color. At the three Sicilian locations the beaches were (from left to right, looking inland from the sea):

At Normandy so many landing craft got broached (turned broadside to the surf), damaged or grounded that it was difficult for follow-on craft to find space to land at the water's edge. The beaches also quickly became littered with damaged or abandoned equipment of all kinds. The 1st InfDiv shoulder patch places this scene on Omaha. Note, top right, a beach marker panel.

*at Licata* Red, Green 1, Green 2, Yellow, Blue
*at Gela* Red, Green, Yellow, Blue, Red 2, Green 2
*at Scoglitti* Red, Green, Yellow, Blue, Green 2, Yellow 2.

This too was confusing; and from Anzio onwards, adjacent beaches were grouped together by phonetic letter code words followed by a color, e.g. at Normandy:

*Omaha* Fox Red, Fox Green, Easy Red, Easy Green, Dog Red, Dog White, Dog Green, Charlie

*Utah* – Uncle Red, Uncle Green, Tare Red, Tare Green

Beaches would be marked by the shore party, which erected 6ft-square colored panels on either flank of the beach topped by the phonetic signal flag.

Beaches could be from 100 to 1,000-plus yards wide, but they were generally between 200 and 500 yards, and able to accommodate two companies landing abreast. Beaches were selected according to surf conditions, gradients, obstacles, exit routes, proximity to the objective, enemy defenses, and availability and types of landing craft.

The "initial beachhead line" was designated inland on the first defendable terrain line, its distance inland depending on terrain, locations of enemy defenses, beach exits, road systems, and nearby seaports and airfields. The beachhead area needed to be large enough to accommodate the many units and masses of supplies that would be arriving.

# THE AMPHIBIOUS ASSAULT

D-Day is the day on which an amphibious assault or other operation commences; and H-Hour is the specific time on D-Day at which an assault commences – when the first landing wave comes ashore. During planning, dates and times of scheduled events were usually specified in relation to D-Day and H-Hour, so that if D-Day or H-Hour were changed to an earlier or later date/time, the planned related events would change accordingly. For example, if D-Day was June 5 and the embarkation of troops was scheduled to begin on the 3rd, it would be

An M4A3 Sherman tank is delivered by an LCT(6), which could carry four of them. Note that the bow rides high; forward bilge tanks have been pumped out and the aft tank flooded, to raise the bow and allow the craft to run closer to shore.

designated in plans to begin on D-2 (D-Day minus two days). If a certain objective ashore was to be secured by June 10, it was specified as D+5 (D-Day plus five days). If D-Day was moved to the 6th – as was the case for Normandy – all dates would shift forward automatically by 24 hours.

The most effective way of discussing the evolution of such operations in the EMTO is simply to examine each of them in turn. **Note, however, that Normandy will not be discussed here**. This may seem to be an illogical omission; but its scope was so vast as to preclude useful summary in a chapter of this length, and specific points based upon examples from that operation are made elsewhere in this text, e.g. in the photo captions and Plates commentaries. The Normandy landings are described in detail in existing Osprey titles.[5]

## North Africa

The invasion of North Africa, Operation "Torch", was for all practical purposes three separate operations executed by three naval task forces. General Dwight Eisenhower was in overall command as Commander, Allied Expeditionary Forces. Returned from six months in Washington as British representative on the Combined Chiefs of Staff Committee, Admiral of the Fleet Sir Andrew Cunningham, as Commander-in-Chief, Mediterranean, was in overall command of naval forces; however, his writ did not run to the Western Naval TF, which landed some 400 miles to the west on Morocco's Atlantic coast – he controlled the Center and Eastern Naval TFs for the Mediterranean landings. Overall planning was conducted by the Joint Chiefs of Staff in London. The Western Naval TF was organized by Commander, Atlantic Amphibious Force on the US East Coast, and landed at three points on the Atlantic coast. It consisted entirely of US Navy forces and 35,000 US Army troops.

[5] See Campaign series No.100, *D-Day 1944: (1) Omaha Beach*, and *Campaign 104, (2): Utah Beach and the US Airborne Landings*; *Campaign 105, (3) Sword Beach and the British Airborne Landings*, and *Campaign 112, (4) Gold and Juno Beaches*.

The Center and Eastern Naval TFs would land on the Mediterranean coast of Algeria at two areas separated by some 200 miles; both these TFs would sail from Britain. The Center Naval TF comprised 39,000 US Army troops borne by Royal Navy ships, and would land on either side of Oran. The Eastern Naval TF contained both US and British ships, with 10,000 US and 23,000 British troops to land on either side of Algiers. The Royal Air Force would provide limited air cover for both TFs. Besides putting combat troops ashore to defeat Vichy French forces, the operation's goal was to secure seaports and establish airbases to support attacks on Axis forces in Tunisia.

Operation "Torch" commenced on November 8, 1942, and was the Allies' first large-scale, multiple-corps, combined amphibious assault. As in the Pacific at this date, dedicated amphibious ships, landing craft and specialized units either did not exist yet or were in short supply. Since the Center and Eastern Naval TFs were largely Royal Navy, we will examine the organization of the American Western Naval TF.

This task force, also designated TF 34, assembled at Norfolk, VA, and Portland, ME, and departed for Morocco on October 24. Overall command was invested in ViceAdm H. Kent Hewitt aboard the USS *Augusta* (CA-31); MajGen Patton commanded the Western Task Force, US Army, with the landing force. TF 34 was organized into three attack groups: Northern at Mehedia and Center at Fedhaia, both northwest of Casablanca; and Southern, southeast of the objective city and port. (For glossary of ship designations, see page 2.)

**Task Force 34 – Western Naval Task Force, Morocco**
*Task Group 34.1 Covering Group* – 1x BB, 2x CA, 4x DD, 1x AO
*Task Group 34.8 Northern Attack Group*
    Fire Support Group – 1x BB, 1x CL
    Transports (60th RCT [+], 9th InfDiv) – 6x AP, 2x AK
    Screen – 5x DD, 1x beacon submarine
    Air Group – 2x ACV, 1x AO
    Air Group Screen – 2x DD
    Special Units – 2x DD, 1x AO, 2x AM, 1x AVP, 1x freighter
*Task Group 34.9 Center Attack Group*
    Fire Support Group – 1x CA, 1x CL
    Control & Fire Support Group – 4x DD
    Transports (3rd InfDiv [+]) – 12x AP, 3x AK
    Screen – 6x DD
    Minecraft – 6x AM
*Task Group 34.2 Air Group* – 1x CV, 1x ACV
    Air Group Screen – 1x CL, 5x DD, 2x beacon submarine, 1x AO
*Task Group 34.10 Southern Attack Group*
    Fire Support Group – 1x BB, 1x CL
    Control & Fire Support Group – 3x DD
    Transports (47th RCT [+], 9th InfDiv) – 5x AP, 1x AK
    Screen – 3x DD
    Assault Destroyers – 2x DD
    Minecraft – 3x AM
    Tankers – 2x AO
    Air Group – 1x ACV
    Air Group Screen – 2x DD
    Other – 1x beacon submarine, 1x tug

Sicily: as MPs escort Italian prisoners along a beach, a 90mm AA gun battery disembarks from an LST over a pontoon causeway. AA units were landed soon after the assault waves to protect the beachhead; they were also employed to engage any counterlanding attempts – i.e. Axis amphibious landings to attack the beachhead – but these were not attempted in the EMTO.

The organization of TF 34 demonstrates the basic elements of a naval amphibious force: an attack group to control all elements for each targeted landing area, with command and control of the force, fire support for shore bombardment, transports for the landing force, minecraft to clear the approaches, screening destroyers for protection against submarines, aircraft and light attack craft; aircraft carriers for close air support and air cover, tankers for refueling, and specialized ships and craft for support and special duties.

This first EMTO amphibious operation was a challenge – nothing approaching this scope and complexity had ever been attempted. The landing units had only minimal training in ship-to-shore operations, and landing craft crews had received only a third of the necessary six months' training. American landing craft consisted of only the LCP(L), LCP(R), LCV and LCM(3). There were no larger landing craft or ships available to land greater numbers of heavy vehicles and troops. It was realized that ramped landing craft were essential. The Navy-inspired commando-type operations directly into seaports mostly failed, and it was understood now that the most cost-effective way of seizing ports was to land on their flanks and invest them from landward.

Cooperation between the Army and the Navy was less than effective. Because of the light opposition it was still felt that night landings were preferable. The Army was more than ever convinced that it should control all landing craft from the point when the Navy transports anchored in the transport area. Many Navy landing craft landed on the wrong beach, often miles from their intended location.

Neither were the Army overly impressed with the naval gunfire support: they believed that pre-arranged barrages were of little use except for a short pre-landing bombardment, and that NGF should be on-call when needed to reduce specific targets. Naval gunfire was critical, however, as it would be at least two hours after H-Hour before light artillery could be landed and ready to fire. Medium artillery would require additional time before it would allow the ground force to operate independent of naval gunfire; realistically, the landing force would rely on NGF until D+1.

The two services used totally separate communications systems, and this resulted in the expanded use of joint liaison teams. The Fifth Army Invasion Training Center was subsequently established at Arzew, Algeria. It not only conducted standard amphibious training and corrected training deficiencies discovered during the landings, but sought to develop new techniques to be used at Sicily and later.

## Sicily

Following the surrender of Axis forces in Tunisia in May 1943, attention was now directed to the underbelly of Axis Europe. Admiral Hewitt, who had commanded the Western Naval Force for North Africa, would command here as well; his headquarters was established in Algiers, with Adm Cunningham's headquarters. Participating Army and Air Forces units were in distant Arzew and Constantine. Air support was a problem. The Allied air forces were attempting to prove that they could defeat the enemy alone, by attacking his airpower and halting his supplies; they had little interest in supporting naval forces and the assault forces in the beachhead, and the air operation was basically conducted independently of the rest of Operation "Husky".

Deception measures led the Axis to believe that the attack might land on Greece or Corsica. Ideally the main landing in Sicily would have been on the coast of the Straits of Messina in the northeast, to cut off the escape of Axis forces to mainland Italy. However, this area and the north coast seaports essential to support the invasion were out of range of North African airbases. and the landings were made in the south. The available assault forces were inadequate: Sicily is a big island, and was defended by two German and six Italian divisions. Planners were torn between capturing two airfields early on, or leaving them in Axis hands and securing two seaports necessary to supply the landing force. With increasing numbers of landing craft and ships, especially the LST and LCI, Army planners thought they might be able to sustain the force with over-the-beach logistics. Either way, there were insufficient forces to prevent the escape northeastward of a withdrawing enemy as the invaders swept around the island's coasts.

The Army still believed at this time that naval gunfire was ineffective against shore targets, but infantry regiments had naval gunfire control parties attached, to direct fire against inland targets. The Air Forces chose to destroy enemy airpower rather than attack beach defenses and "seal off the beachhead" from enemy counterattacks. In the event, the defenses were so weak that no supporting bombardment was necessary.

**Anzio, January 22, 1944: an LST comes under attack by Luftwaffe bombers.**

The Navy and Air Forces would achieve sea and air superiority, and attack enemy airbases. The landing would be before dawn, supported for the first time by parachute and glider landings. Rather than capturing seaports as the initial objective, the main goal finally decided upon was to secure three airfields. The US Western Naval TF would deliver Patton's Seventh Army on the lower southwest coast of Sicily just above the island's southern tip; some British ships and craft were also assigned. The British Eastern Naval TF would land on the east coast just above the southern tip. As it had been for Morocco, the Western Naval TF was divided into three forces, but this time named after their landing sites. The task force staged from several bases in Tunisia beginning on July 8, 1943, and followed complex deceptive routes before rushing north from Malta to land on the 10th.

**Task Force 80 – Western Naval Task Force**
*Task Group 80.1* Force Flagship Group – 1x APA, 1x DD
*Task Group 80.2* Escort Group – 9x DD
*Task Group 80.3*
    Screening Group – 1x DD, 15x PT
    Demonstration Group (Beach Jumpers) – 1x PT, 8x ASR boat
*Task Group 80.5* Minelaying Group – 3x minelayer
*Task Group 80.6*
    Reserve Group (18th RCT, 1st InfDiv; 2nd ArmdDiv [–])
    – 2x AP, 7x freighter, 6x LST, 27x LCI
**Task Force 86 – Licata Attack Force ("Joss")**
    – 1x AVP, 1x DD (3rd InfDiv [–])
*Task Group 86.1* Support Group – 2x CL, 2x DD, 1x SS, 1x PC
*Task Group 86.2* Gaffi Attack Group
    – 1x DD, 5x fire support craft, 1x AM
    Landing & Control Craft – 7x LST, 15x LCI, 21x LCT, 2x PC, 5x SC
*Task Group 86.3* Molla Task Group
    – 1x DD, 1x LST, 1x fire support craft, 1x AM
    Landing & Control Craft – 2x LSI, 6x LST, 1x LCI, 3x LCT, 2x PC, 5x SC
*Task Group 86.4* Salso Attack Group – 1x DD, 5x fire support craft
    Landing & Control Craft – 12x LST, 1x LCI, 25x LCT, 2x PC, 5x SC
*Task Group 86.5* Falconara Attack Group – 1x DD, 4x fire support craft
    Landing & Control Craft – 10x LST, 16x LCI, 9x LCT, 4x SC, 1x PC
*Task Group 86.7* Salvage Group – 2x tug

**Task Force 81 – Gela Attack Force ("Dime")**
Beach Identification Group – 1x SS, 1x PC
*Task Group 81.2* Transport Group (1st InfDiv [–])
 – 7x AP, 2x LSI, 17x LCI, 3x PC, 4x SC
*Task Group 81.3* LST Group – 14x LST
*Task Group 81.4* LCI Group – 16x LCI
*Task Group 81.5* Fire Support Group – 2x CL, 2x DD
*Task Group 81.6* Screen – 10x DD
*Task Group 81.7* Control Group – 4x PC, 5x SC
*Task Group 81.8* Sweeper Group – 7x AM
*Task Group 81.9* Salvage Group – 1x salvage vessel, 4x tug
**Task Force 85 – Scoglitti Attack Group ("Cent")**
*Task Group 85.1* Attack Group One – 1x AGC, 2x DD, 1x SS
 Transports (45th InfDiv [–]) – 12x AP, 8x LST, 6x LCI, 6x LCT, 2x tug
 Screen – 3x DD, 4x PC, 2x SC
 Minecraft – 9x AM
*Task Group 85.2* Attack Group Two
 Transports (45th InfDiv reserve) – 6x AP, 5x LST
 Screen – 4x DD, 2x PC, 2x SC
 Minecraft – 5x AM
*Task Group 85.3* Fire Support Group – 1x CL, 1x monitor, 7x DD
**Task Force 87** Train – 5x auxiliaries, 7x AO

Each of the three landing forces landed on four or five beaches, the three areas separated by 3–5 miles, before dawn on July 10. Resistance was heavy to light depending on the specific site. Counterattacks were quickly launched by the enemy, but naval gunfire contributed to their defeat. Some ships were lost to air attacks in spite of the AAF effort to maintain air superiority. The major problem with the landings was the sandbars blocking the approach of LSTs; there was also difficulty in deploying pontoons, which were in short supply, and delayed unloading due to shortage of labor troops. There were notably fewer squabbles between the Army and Navy, the sailors having grasped that they were there to transport and support the landing forces. There were difficulties with over-the-beach logistics, but the lessons learned had a definite influence on the planning for Normandy.

Two subsidiary landings were made on Sicily's north coast in failed attempts to block enemy withdrawal: on August 8, 2nd Bn, 30th Infantry from 3rd InfDiv landed at Sant'Agata, and on the 16th the 157th Infantry, 45th InfDiv landed at Barcelona.

The airborne phase of the Sicily operation failed badly, with heavy casualties from misdropping and friendly fire; the details are outside the scope of this study.[6]

## Salerno

The invasion of Sicily was considered more as a conclusion to the securing of North Africa than as a stepping stone towards Italy. It was feared by many that an invasion of mainland Italy might delay the eventually inevitable cross-Channel attack on occupied France; but it was finally decided that an invasion of Italy could knock that country out of the war, and usefully force Germany to divert troops to fill the void

---

[6] See Elite 136, *World War II Airborne Warfare Tactics*

*Anzio, January 22, 1944: troops of the US 3rd InfDiv disembark from LCI(L)s – note early square bridges and side gangways – while a bombed craft burns in the background. LCIs were not used in the initial assault waves, but were well suited to delivering reserve companies – see Plate C.*

left by the extensive demobilized Italian forces in Greece and the Balkans. The arguments bounced back and forth, and it was not until Mussolini's fall in July 1943 that the decision was made to land – at Salerno, near the "instep" of the Italian boot just south of the key port of Naples.

While directed to conduct Operation "Avalanche" with available assets, Gen Eisenhower requested 40 additional transports – at a time when the Pacific had a dire need for more. The Western Naval TF (TF 80) would again deliver the mostly American Southern Attack Force and the mainly British Northern Attack Force. Planning was rushed; Sicily had not been secured until a month before the Salerno landing. Not only would air support fly from Sicily, but five carriers were available; this was important, as the Luftwaffe was still very active and even attacking staging ports in Tunisia. Rather than staging from Sicily, within easy Axis bombing and air reconnaissance range, most of the invasion fleet staged from Oran, Algiers, Bizerta and Tripoli, though some did depart from Palermo and Termini in Sicily.

Prior to the landing British troops made several small landings on Italy's "toe" to draw Axis troops away from Salerno; these were launched across the Messina Strait from Sicily during September 3–8, 1943. Italian officials signed a covert armistice with the Allies, which Eisenhower announced at 1830 hours, September 8 – nine hours before the Salerno landing.

Most of the American Southern Attack Force departed Oran on September 5; the fleet made its run into Salerno Bay on the night of the 8th, and the landings took place before dawn on the 9th. The American landing was on the southern side of the broad bay on four tightly bunched beaches, with the British landing to the north.

**Task Force 81 Southern Attack Force**
*Task Group 81.5* Fire Support Group – 4x CL, 1x monitor, 3x DD
*Task Group 81.6* Screen – 11x DD
*Task Group 81.2* Transport Group (36th InfDiv[+])
 – 18x transports, 3x LST
*Task Group 81.3* Landing Craft Group – 27x LST, 32x LCI, 6x LCT

*Task Group 81.7* Control Group – 8x PC, 4x fire support craft
*Task Group 81.8* Minesweeper Group – 21x AM
*Task Group 81.9* Salvage Group – 2x tugs
*Task Group 80.2* Picket Group – 16x PT
*Task Group 80.4* Diversion Group
  – 7x PT, 4x SC, 1x gunboat, 10x ASR craft

German resistance was fairly heavy, and supported by more insistent air attacks than previously experienced. A tank counterattack was beaten off by ground troops and naval gunfire. Despite this resistance the US troops soon reached their assembly areas less than 1,000 yards inland. Naval gunfire proved valuable in making the landing "stick", as German counterattacks were continuous for over a week. It was some time before the beachhead line, intended to be secured on D-Day and several miles inland, was finally reached. The situation was serious enough that on September 12 planning began to extract either the US or the British force and lift it to the north. An amphibious withdrawal while actually engaged is the most difficult of operations, and fortunately it was not attempted. The Allied build-up continued and a breakout was finally achieved, with Naples secured on October 1. The Diversion Group remained active to the north of Naples to hold German defenders there. The lack of a seaport had hampered the build-up and everything had to come over the beach. This lodgment served to establish a solid foothold in Italy, and the Fifth Army began to push north, slowed by successive German defensive lines in strong mountain positions.

## Anzio

The Anglo-American push north to Rome was stalled on the Gustav Line across central Italy by December 1943. In an effort to break the stalemate planning had begun for Operation "Shingle" in late November. This was to be an outflanking amphibious assault aimed at Anzio, 37 miles south of Rome and 60 miles behind the troublesome Gustav Line. The operation kept being delayed in hopes that the land advance would make headway. At one point Gen Eisenhower was

**In the EMTO the exploitation of a beachhead for large-scale ground operations depended upon the early capture of a port which could accept heavy shipping. The Axis troops always destroyed harbor facilities as thoroughly as possible before withdrawing, and it took much time and major resources to repair them and get ports back into operation. Army engineer special brigades, engineer combat and construction battalions and quartermaster port battalions were employed in this massive task. Here 5-ton crawler cranes clear debris; the same equipment was also used to unload cargo from landing craft and barges.**

ordered to send all 90 of his LSTs to Britain, but he was allowed to retain 68 of them. With Eisenhower appointed to oversee the Normandy landing, many senior commanders in the Mediterranean were changed.

By the end of December 1943, with the Allies bogged down at the foot of Monte Cassino, the Anzio operation was resurrected. Only three weeks were allowed for planning and mounting the operation. Rear Admiral Frank Lowry, commanding 8th Amphibious Force, would be the naval commander, and D-Day was set for January 22, 1944; Lowry was allowed to retain – briefly – some landing vessels scheduled to sail for Britain. Only one US and one British division would be landed, although six would be needed to hold the beachhead.

The British Eighth Army on the east side of Italy would apply enough pressure to prevent the Germans from shifting troops to the west to respond to the operation. It was hoped that the landing itself would drain German reserves from in front of the Fifth US Army in the west half of the peninsula, and cut the supply line from Rome. The Air Forces attempted to seal off the beachhead area; although unsuccessful, they did manage to ground German reconnaissance aircraft, which prevented the task force's approach from being detected. The US 3rd InfDiv staged from Pozzuoli and the British 1st Div from Salerno; only limited rehearsals were possible. TF 81 sailed on January 21, ten days after the Fifth Army offensive commenced; this made slow progress as German reserves were poured in, and the Americans advanced only 10 miles.

The actual landing on the 22nd met with little resistance. The Americans – X-Ray Force – landed 2 miles southeast of Anzio on two adjacent beaches, and the British – Peter Force – 5 miles to the northwest.

**Task Force 81** – 1x CL, 1x DE
*Task Group 81.2* Ranger Group – 2x LSI, 2x LST, 1x LCI, 3x LCT, 3x SC
**X-Ray Force**
*Task Group 81.3* Red Beach Group
  – 12x LST, 31x LCI, 22x LCT, 4x PC, 6x SC, 3x fire support craft
*Task Group 81.4* Green Beach Group
  – 1x LSI, 17x LCI, 11x LCT, 2x PC, 2x SC, 3x fire support craft
*Task Group 81.5* First Follow-on Group – 39x LST, 20x LCI, 6x LCT
*Task Group 81.6* Escort Group – 5x DD, 2x DE, 2x AM
*Task Group 81.7* Sweeper Group – 22x AM, 1x SC
*Task Group 81.8* Gunfire Support Group – 2x CL, 5x DD

The Allied landing forces secured Anzio, linked up quickly, and occupied the initial beachhead line. Within days German counter-attacks, air attacks, and foul weather slowed the build-up. By January 28 the Germans had completely contained the beachhead in a lodgment measuring about 19 by 4 miles. The landing force stayed there – under siege and heavy bombardment, and draining resources needed elsewhere in Italy – until finally able to break out in mid-April 1944 in conjunction with the Allied breakthrough at Cassino.[7]

## Southern France

Consideration of plans for the last large EMTO amphibious operation began in 1943. Some leaders wavered over its necessity, but eventually its benefits were recognized. A landing on the French Riviera coast would

---
[7] See Campaign 155, *Anzio 1944*

Seen from the stern, an LCM(3) heads for shore loaded with assault troops. Many "Mike boats" were not provided with machine guns, but here a pair of tarpaulin-shrouded .50cal M2 MGs on Mk 21 pedestal mounts can be seen flanking the central raised pilot house.

implement a pincer movement against the Germans, hold German units in the south and even drawing others there, thus keeping them out of the main battle in northern France. Trained US divisions in the States were prepared for deployment to Europe, but what Channel ports had been secured, and the overstretched over-the-beach logistics, were inadequate to bring them in to the northern front; they could be fed into France by landing on the Mediterranean coast, as could the newly organized and trained Free French divisions in North Africa. Such landings would additionally provide a route to enter southern Germany.

Originally designated Operation "Anvil", it was redesignated "Dragoon" because of possible compromise. German coastal defenses were relatively weak when compared to Normandy, but efforts were underway to strengthen them. Even though the Germans were expecting a landing on the south coast the massive battles in Normandy inevitably pulled units north, and by D-Day – August 15, 1944 – only a token defense force remained.

The Western Naval Task Force was again commanded by ViceAdm H.Kent Hewitt. Three beachheads were selected on a 45-mile stretch of coast, with one US division landing on each. The US/Canadian First Special Service Force would secure the Iles de Hyéres on the western flank, and a US/British provisional airborne division would be delivered inland. The Free French made efforts to include large units in the initial landing, but insufficient shipping existed; they would land soon afterwards further west and would secure the important ports of Toulon and Marseilles, key objectives of the operation. Amphibious training and

At Normandy, where it was realistically assumed that the major port of Cherbourg could not be seized and made operational for some time after the landings, great efforts went into developing and building artificial harbors off the Allied beaches. Off Omaha this was accomplished by scuttling ships and bringing floating breakwaters and piers over from England. Here landing craft tie up to Gooseberry No.2 (the codename differentiated it from the British Mulberry harbors). AA gun crews were retained aboard the scuttled ships, and landing craft crews could obtain rations and water from them.

rehearsals were conducted at Salerno, but under such time pressure that one of the task force commanders, fearing his forces were not ready and begging Hewitt to postpone D-Day, took his own life.

Built up by the transfer of amphibious ships no longer needed in the Channel after Normandy, this was by far the largest amphibious operation in the Mediterranean, with 880 ships (indeed, even in the Pacific only three amphibious operations were larger). A large number of British and French ships were assigned to the task force. "Dragoon" saw few innovations, though 41 Underwater Demolition Teams, each with 11 men, were employed in the MTO for the first time.

**Western Naval Task Force**
Control Force – 1x ACG, 9x AM
Special Operations Group (diversionary)
    – 1x DD, 12x PT, 3x gunboat, 3x fighter directions ship
*Task Force 86 Sitka Force* (1st Spl Svc Force)
     Fire Support Group – 1x BB, 1x CA, 3x CL, 4x DD
     Transport Group – 5x destroyer-transport, 5x LSI, 17x PT, 5x AM
*Task Force 84 Alpha Force* (3rd InfDiv[+])
     – 1x Coast Guard cutter, 1x fighter control ship
     Assault Groups – 2x AP, 3x AKA, 3x freighters, 25x LST, 55x LCI, 60x LCT, 20x LCM, 8x AM, 9x PC, 12x fire support craft, 10x LCC
     Gunfire Support Group – 1x BB, 1x CA, 5x CL, 6x DD
     Minesweeper Group – 30x AM, 6x SC, 2x LCC
*Task Force 85 Delta Force* (45th InfDiv[+])
     – 1x seaplane tender, 1x DD, 1x fighter direction tender
     Transport Group – 6x AP, 2x freighter, 1x LSI, 23x LST, 49x LCI, 48x LCT, 8x LCM, 8x fire support craft, 5x LCC, 6x SC
     Gunfire Support Group – 2x BB, 6x CL, 8x DD
     Minesweeper Group – 10x AM
     Salvage & Firefighting Group – 6x tug
*Task Force 87 Camel Force* (36th InfDiv[+]) – 1x AK
     Assault Groups – 3x AP, 2x AKA, 3x freighter, 21x LST, 1x LSI, 29x

LCI, 45x LCT, 4x LCM, 7x fire support craft, 7x LCC, 17x SC, 16x PC
Bombardment Group – 1x BB, 1x CA, 5x CL, 11x DD
Minesweeper Group – 31x AM
Salvage & Firefighting Group – 6x tug, 3x LCI, 1x LCT, 4x LCM

*Task Force 88 Aircraft Carrier Force*
9x carrier, 4x CLAA, 53x DD, 6x DE, 7x corvette

The various task forces staged from Brindisi, Taranto and Naples, Italy; Palermo, Sicily; and Oran, Algeria, departing in the second week of August. On the night of August 14 all arrived off the west coast of Corsica, then headed northwest to the French coast some 50 miles west of the Italian border. There was resistance in some sectors, but overall it was a comparatively easy landing; indeed, it is frequently described as an almost perfect amphibious operation.

\* \* \*

From the early operations in the Mediterranean, when there were barely enough landing craft for the infantry, and insufficient capacity to land tanks and heavy equipment, American amphibious doctrine and capability had evolved dramatically. By August 1944 there was more than enough shipping, beaching vessels, specialized amphibious support units, perfected naval gunfire support, and other resources available. Logistical capabilities, coordination, command and control had all been greatly improved. The Normandy landings were the largest, most ambitious and most dangerous the world had seen, and had succeeded despite strong enemy defenses and determined opposition. The organization of amphibious operations in the EMTO had evolved in somewhat different ways than those developed by the Navy-dominated Pacific Theater; but the post-war joint command structure adopted by the new Department of Defense would be based on that of the Pacific.

# FURTHER READING

Baker, A.D. II (introd), *Allied Landing Craft of World War Two* (Annapolis, MD; Naval Institute Press, 1985. Originally published as *Allied Landing Craft and Ships*, ON1226, 1944)

Bruce, Colin J., *Invaders: British and American Experience of Seaborne Landings 1939–45* (London; Chatham Publishing, 1999)

Clifford, Kenneth J., *Amphibious Warfare Development in Britain and America 1920–1940* (New York; Edgewood, 1983)

Coll, Blanche D., Jean E.Keith & Herbert H.Rosenthal, *United States Army in World War II: The Corps of Engineers: Troops and Equipment* (Washington, DC; US Govt Printing Office, 1988)

Friedman, Norman, *US Amphibious Ships and Craft: An Illustrated Design History* (Annapolis, MD; Naval Institute Press, 2002)

Gawne, Jonathan, *Spearheading D-Day: American Special Units of the Normandy Invasion* (Paris; Histoire & Collections, 1998)

Stanton, Shelby L., *World War II Order of Battle: An Encyclopedic Reference to US Army Ground Forces from Battalion through Division, 1939–1946* (Revised Edition) (Mechanicsburg, PA; Stackpole Books, 2006)

Strahan, Jerry E., *Andrew Jackson Higgins and the Boats That Won World War II* (New Orleans, LA; Louisiana State University Press, 1994)

# THE PLATES

## A: LANDING CRAFT
(The British LCA is included here, as it was used to deliver US troops.) Most US craft employed in the MTO and ETO were finished in haze-gray or a similar shade, and British craft in the Channel in a pale blue scheme. These colors were too light, and any illumination allowed the detection of the craft at night against dark water. Hull numbers were mostly white, but black was also used, especially in the Mediterranean. Smaller craft carried aboard attack transports (APA) and attack cargo ships (AKA) were identified by the parent ship's type code – minus the first "A" for Auxiliary – and hull number, followed by the landing craft number. American landing craft often bore a "US" prefix one-third to twice as large as the hull number; British craft did not carry such nationality letters. LCTs and larger landing vessels were assigned BuShips hull numbers.

The data listed below for each type are the year of introduction; numbers built; length x beam; armament; crew + passengers; cargo and vehicle capacity; and a typical hull number, as illustrated:

**1: Landing Craft, Personnel (Large) – LCP(L)**
1941; 2,193; 36ft 3in × 10ft 10in; 2x .30cal; 3 + 36; 4 tons; "PA-20-4"

**2: Landing Craft, Personnel (Ramp) – LCP(R)**
1942; 2,631; 36ft 3in × 10ft 10in; 2x .30cal; 3 + 36; 4 tons; "PA 1612"

**3: Landing Craft, Vehicle – LCV**
1942; 2,366; 36ft 3in × 10ft 10in; 1x .30cal; 3 + 36; 5 tons – 1x light gun or 1x 1-ton truck + 12 troops; "KA 13-14"

**4: Landing Craft, Vehicle and Personnel – LCVP**
1942; 23,358; 35ft 10in × 10ft 6in; 2x .30cal; 3 + 36; 4 tons – 1x light gun or 1x 1-ton truck + 12 troops; "PA 33-4"

**5: Landing Craft, Assault – LCA (British)**
1939; unknown; 41ft 6in × 10ft; 2/3 x .303; 4 + 35 + 800lb; "LCA 1237"

**6: Landing Craft, Mechanized Mk III – LCM(3)**
1942; 8,631; 50ft × 14ft 1in; 2x .50cal; 4 + 60; 30 tons or 1x medium tank or 1x medium gun; "PA6-2"

**7: Landing Craft, Mechanized Mk VI – LCM(6)**
1943; 2,718; 56ft × 14ft 1in; 2x .50cal; 4 + 75; 35 tons or 1x medium tank or 1x medium gun; "PA-22-20"

**8: Landing Craft, Tank Mk V – LCT(5)**
1942; 500; 114ft 2in × 32ft 8in; 2x 20mm; 11; 150 tons or 4x light tanks or 3x medium tanks or 9x trucks; "33"

**9: Landing Craft, Tank Mk VI – LCT(6)**
1943; 965; 119ft 1in × 32ft 8in; 2x 20mm; 13; 150 tons or 4x light tanks or 3x medium tanks or 10x trucks; "US[673]"

**10: Landing Craft, Infantry (Large) – LCI(L) – LCI-1 Class**
1942; 1,031; 158ft 6in × 23ft 8in; 4x 20mm; 24 + 188 or 75 tons; "US [92]"

**11: Landing Craft, Infantry (Large) – LCI(L) – LCI-351 Class**
1943; 605; 158ft 6in × 23ft 8in; 5x 20mm; 29 + 209 or 75 tons; "369"

## B: ASSAULT BOAT TEAM
**Normandy, June 6, 1944**
(Note that this illustration is diagrammatic; for clear separation of the various groups embarked, the overhead view shows the troops slightly smaller than true scale.)

A boat team or assault section was essentially half a rifle platoon augmented with additional elements; an officer led each section, with an NCO assistant. There was a great deal of variation in the composition of boat teams between individual units and particular landing operations. The normal Browning Automatic Rifle (BAR) and bazooka teams each had four men and two weapons; but for a landing, in two of a company's assault sections – as illustrated in this example – the teams were halved, and a four-man team with an M1919A4 .30cal light machine gun was substituted.

Six landing craft carried a company's three rifle platoons, and a seventh craft the company command group and attached personnel – forward observers, medics, gapping teams, and guides and liaison personnel for following units. The battalion heavy weapons company would be organized into six support boat teams, each consisting of: rifle team (5 riflemen); heavy machine gun team (6 men, 1x M1917A1 .30cal MG); wire-cutting team (4 riflemen with bangalore torpedoes and wire-cutters); demolition team (5 riflemen with

*Troops of a follow-up wave at Normandy wade ashore from LCVPs; vehicles are stalled at the water's edge, waiting for obstacles and mines to be cleared. At left, a GI carries a mine detector, and at right another has a bazooka waterproofed with a plastic bag. The horizontal white bar painted on the back of the helmet identifies an NCO; officers displayed a vertical bar. See Plate B.*

satchel and pole charges); and mortar team (8 men, 1x M1 81mm mortar).

The official scale of weapons and munitions carried by the assault team illustrated were as follows:

**1:** Assault section leader (carbine; 1x fragmentation grenade, 1x white phosphorus grenade, 6x colored smoke grenades)
**2:** Rifle team (5x rifles; 7x frag grenades, 3x WP grenades, 10x rifle grenades, 1x bangalore torpedo)
**3:** Wire-cutting team (4x rifles; 2x WP grenades, 2x bangalore torpedoes)
**4:** BAR team (1x rifle, 1x BAR; 27x BAR magazines)
**5:** Bazooka team (1x rifle, 1x carbine, 1x bazooka; 18x bazooka rounds)
**6:** Mortar team (1x pistol, 3x carbines, 1x M2 60mm mortar; 36x mortar rounds)
**7:** Light machine gun team (1x pistol, 3x carbines, 1x LMG; 1,250 rounds for LMG)
**8:** Flamethrower team (1x pistol, 1x rifle, 1x flamethrower; 6x frag grenades, 4x WP grenades)
**9:** Demolition team (4x rifles; 8x satchel charges, 3x pole charges, 6x TNT blocks; 4x frag grenades, 4x WP grenades)
**10:** Assistant section leader (rifle; 8 x frag grenades, 2x WP grenades)
**11:** Medical aidman (pistol)

## C: LANDING CRAFT, INFANTRY (LARGE)

The LCI(L) was developed quickly in 1942. It was designed for short-range shore-to-shore operations only, which made it more useful in the Mediterranean and the Channel than in the Pacific. LCIs saw their first use in the Mediterranean during the Sicily landings of July 1943. Their simple troop accommodations and food and water restrictions limited their potential transit time; they could and did travel long distances when necessary, but were designed to accommodate troops for a maximum of 48 hours.

Here, unopposed troops disembark on a Mediterranean beach down the port side 36ft gangway; to deploy the gangways, they were slid forwards off the side sponsons and lowered by tackle from the I-beam catheads extended overhead. The troops emerged from their below-deck compartments protected by side bulkheads, and an entire rifle company could disembark in under five minutes.

Landing craft were well armed for antiaircraft defense; this weaponry also provided fire support, and made the craft useful for screening transport areas from fast attack boats. The LCI was armed with five Oerlikon Mk IV 20mm automatic cannons, one on the bow and one on each corner of the deckhouse. After the first landing wave was ashore, landing craft gunners were prohibited from firing at shore targets unless an enemy weapon firing on them was positively detected – otherwise there was a high risk of firing into previously landed troops. The 20mm hammered out 550 rounds per minute, requiring the 60-round magazine to be changed every eight seconds.

## D: GAP-CLEARING

Gap-clearing parties were typically landed in the third to fifth waves; the assault wave landing craft had to make it through the array of obstacles on their own. The gap-clearing parties were responsible for clearing paths for larger, less maneuverable craft to land vehicles, and to allow vehicles to move inland, by destroying beach obstacles including those exposed by a falling tide. The teams were organized differently for each operation; they might comprise Army combat engineers, Navy Seabees and/or shore battalion personnel, or men from naval combat demolition units (NCDUs), as depicted here. In Normandy joint gap-clearing parties were formed from available organizations; parties might consist of from six to more than 20 men, using a wide variety of demolition devices.

**1:** The "demolitioner" in the foreground is rigging a satchel charge **(inset, 2)** to a steel "hedgehog" obstacle. The charge contains eight 2½lb M2 tetrytol demolition blocks, linked together by detonating cord at 8in intervals to form an M1 chain demolition charge. The blocks measure 2in × 2in × 11in; the 20lb of explosive, slightly more powerful than TNT, are more than sufficient to blow the "hedgehog" apart. The charge will be detonated by a short length of delay fuse ignited by a waterproof M2 fuse lighter activated with a pull ring.
**3:** Another NCDU member in the background is fixing four ½lb TNT blocks to a post obstacle topped by a Tellermine 43 – capable of blowing the bows off an LCVP. The TNT block **(inset, 4)** is fitted with a 30-second delay fuse ignited by a non-waterproof M1 fuse lighter – this was sometimes waterproofed by means of a condom. Some assault troops carried these in order to blast starter-holes for digging foxholes. Fuse lighters, delay fuses and detonators were carried separate from the charges.

In the background a D-8 armored bulldozer has arrived; these – like dozer-tanks – proved to be invaluable for simply bulldozing de-mined obstacles out of the way.

One of the DD Shermans from Co A, 70th Tank Bn was hit by an antitank gun on Exit 2, one of the narrow causeways leading inland through the flooded areas behind Utah Beach. The canvas floatation screen was collapsed around the hull as soon as the DD tanks came ashore; other photos from Normandy show that many crews simply hacked off the skirt at the earliest opportunity. See Plate E.

## E: M4A1 SHERMAN DUPLEX-DRIVE TANK

Kept secret in order to achieve surprise in the Normandy landings, the DD was an M4A1 fitted with a special transmission that could transfer power to either the tracks, or two aft-mounted 18in propellers giving a water speed of 4 miles per hour. To provide floatation a collapsible skirt of rubberized canvas was fitted; this was erected using stays and braces, to rise just above the level of the turret top. Once ashore, the propellers could be raised, and the skirt lowered to lie folded around the track guards. The weapons could not be fired with the floatation skirt raised. The sea had to be calm, as the skirt bracing could not withstand much pounding and there was less than a foot of freeboard at the skirt top. A jettisonable launching gear framework was fitted to the bow to prevent the skirt collapsing on impact with the water when the four tanks launched from each LCT.

**1:** The tank heads for the beach. The commander, standing on a small platform fixed behind the turret top and holding a grab bar, could steer by altering the angle of the propellers by means of a vertical lever.

**2:** The commander climbs down as the tank comes ashore; the inside of the skirt shows reinforcement and repair patches.

**3:** The skirt has been lowered and the propellers raised.

Three US tank battalions (70th, 741st & 743rd) were equipped with DD tanks for the Normandy landings; they were issued to two companies in each, to be launched 5,000–6,000 yards off shore to swim ahead of the landing craft waves. The battalions' Co As and the M5 light tanks of their Co Ds were fitted with fording kits (see Plate F); dozer-tanks were included in this wave, which would be landed later to make only a short wade ashore. The DDs and other early-arriving tanks were employed as assault guns to knock out German emplacements, and they achieved mixed results.

In rough conditions, the 70th held back its DDs until they were only 1,500 yards off shore, and 28 reached Utah Beach unscathed (four were lost when their LCT was sunk by a mine). Most of the 743rd's tanks, also held back because of the sea conditions, were landed directly on Omaha Beach by LCTs; but only five from the 741st made it ashore, of which three were landed directly. Of the 32 DDs which attempted to swim in to Omaha, 27 were swamped by a combination of wind, waves and a strong cross-current; 33 crewmen were drowned, and only two tanks reached the beach under their own power.

(The British 27th Armd Bde assigned one battalion of DDs to each British and Canadian beach – from 4th/7th Dragoon Guards, East Riding Yeomanry and 13th/18th Hussars, from west to east. Launching off the westernmost Gold Beach was prevented by rough seas, and the tanks were carried to shore by their LCTs; on Juno, some DDs were launched from only 1,000 yards and others were landed directly; but 31 of 40 tanks launched 5,000 yards out made it safely to Sword Beach.)

## F: LCM AND SHERMAN RIGGED FOR FORDING

A system of fording kits for tanks was developed in time for the North Africa landings of November 1942, and subsequently other versions were produced. For tanks, all openings in the hull were sealed with a waterproof compound, and large, hooded, forward air intake and rear exhaust stacks were mounted on the engine deck. The M4 Sherman used the MT-S kit, which was used on later models in conjunction with the MT-1 to MT-4 kits for the M4A1 to M4A4 respectively. Fording kits were fitted to tanks even if the landing craft were expected to be able to drop their ramps on dry beach – there were simply too many factors that might prevent craft from beaching near shore, and since it was essential for tanks to get ashore as soon as possible, they were prepared for all eventualities. One tactic was for tanks wading ashore to remain hull-deep in the water with the deck almost awash, and provide fire support with the turret guns while the water protected the hulls from return fire (when the turret was rotated or the mantlet elevated the waterproof seals would break.)

The 50ft-long LCM(3) and the 56ft LCM(6) were essential craft whose utility went far beyond landing a single medium tank. They were ideal for landing 155mm howitzers, AA guns, bulldozers, cargo trucks, and other heavy equipment needed in the early waves, while still being small and maneuverable enough to present a comparatively difficult target. They could carry up to 60 troops, allowing them to bring in follow-on units such as reserve companies, gap-clearing parties, engineers and medical teams. Once the main body was ashore these "Mike boats" shuttled additional cargo and vehicles to the beach, evacuated casualties and served as general purpose utility craft.

*View forward inside an LCVP carrying infantry of the 16th RCT from 1st InfDiv towards Fox and Easy sectors of Omaha Beach on the morning of June 6, 1944; see Plate H. The failure of the preliminary air and naval bombardments to silence the strong German gun positions dominating Omaha, and the swamping of nearly all their DD tanks, condemned the initial assault waves from 1st and 29th InfDivs to very heavy casualties on Omaha. At Utah, the 8th RCT from 4th InfDiv suffered very light losses: a lucky navigational error landed them some 2,000 yards from the intended location, on a stretch with far fewer obstacles; the ground above the beach was much lower; the preliminary bombardment had shattered the defenses, and most of the DD tanks landed successfully.*

## G: ACROSS-THE-BEACH TRACKWAYS

The ability to move heavy vehicles across the short distance from the landing craft ramp to firm ground was critical to the success or failure of a landing force in gaining a foothold on the enemy shore. Wheeled and tracked vehicles would churn up even packed sand, soon making lanes to the beach exits impassable. Following vehicles could not simply make additional lanes without the time-consuming task of clearing more obstacles and minefields. Various types of matting were therefore used to reduce the destruction of vehicle lanes.

Two types were provided in 10ft-wide, 25ft-long rolls. Sommerfield trackway **(1)** was a wire-like mesh reinforced by crosswise semi-flexible narrow gauge rods. Chespaling trackway was made of canvas reinforced with closely spaced wooden palings or slats; and 30in to 36in-wide rolls of burlap were sometimes laid beneath Sommerfield (neither illustrated here). Airfield matting was also employed: square-mesh track (SMT) was a semi-flexible heavy steel 3in square mesh **(2)** issued in $7\frac{1}{2}$ ft-wide rolls **(3)**; sections were fastened together with metal clips **(inset, 4)**. Marston matting or pierced steel planks (PSP) were perforated panels 15in wide × 10ft long **(5)**, locking together at the edges by tabs and slots. Wire-bound wooden slat mats 3ft wide **(6)** were available for foot troops, and two laid parallel could support vehicles. Once the landing force was firmly established, rock quarries were opened by engineer units using portable rock-crushers, draglines and shovel-loaders, and gravel roads were laid across beaches. Here, a Seabee **(7)** wearing a faded Navy deck jacket sledge-hammers hooked iron stakes to secure Sommerfield tracking, while an Army shore party combat engineer **(8)** hammers clips to fasten lengths of SMT together. In the distance, a beached Rhino ferry **(9)** assembled from pontoons is about to discharge a cargo of vehicles.

## H: THE ASSAULT WAVES

The organization of assault waves varied greatly, not just between specific operations but between units in the same operation. This depended on the extent and type of operation expected, the density of obstacles, and the terrain beyond the beach in different sectors. If numerous and heavy fortifications were expected, tanks would be landed as soon as possible to serve as assault guns – they were seldom needed to fight off enemy tank counterattacks, but were available if required. Infantry normally had to go in first, but in some cases tanks were landed on their heels, or even ahead of them. Close behind the infantry and tanks came the gap assault or demolition parties to clear obstacles and mines. Reserve companies would soon follow, with light AA and AT guns, more engineers, medical aid stations and assault command posts.

These waves typically landed at ten-minute intervals, but there might be a 30-minute gap between the landing of leading assault companies, tanks and gapping teams, and that of the reserve companies. This allowed the assault troops to clear immediate opposition and gain a foothold, rather than having follow-on waves landing immediately on to a fire-swept beach. Artillery would be ashore after one-and-a-half or two hours; behind the guns came DUKWs with ammunition for immediate use, but it might take another hour or more before they were in firing positions. Close behind the lead waves were salvage craft, and bulldozers would be landed from Rhino ferries to clear damaged landing craft and to help retract those which had broached or were hard aground.

This plate depicts the *planned* landing of the first three waves on Easy Green sector of Omaha Beach, Normandy, on June 6, 1944. The beach was protected by Element C obstacles and a line of stakes, then by log antiboat ramps, and behind those by steel "hedgehogs". **Wave 1**, shown here at the edge of the water, was to land at H-Hour (0630hrs): four LCTs each carrying three Shermans – one with a dozer-blade – from Co A, 743rd Tank Bn would in this case land one minute ahead of the infantry. Fitted with fording stacks, the tanks would still be disembarking as the infantry passed them. At H+1 minute **Wave 2** of six LCVPs would bring in Co E, 2nd Bn, 116th Infantry, organized into assault sections of 30-plus men. At H+3 minutes they would be followed by **Wave 3**: two LCMs would land gap assault teams of 27 soldiers from Co C, 146th Engineer Bn, and 14 sailors from NCDUs 137 and 140. Each LCM also carried a dozer-Sherman and two rubber boats each with 500lb of demolitions equipment. There would then be a 27-minute break to allow the gap teams to clear obstacles, before the arrival of the command element of Co E, 2/116th in an LCVP; part of Co H (Weapons) in two LCVPs; and AA guns in another two.

That was the plan; the *reality* was very different. On D-Day, Co E, 2/116th were landed 2,000–3,000 yards to the east on another regiment's beaches; most of the tanks were hit by concentrated German fire as they struggled to cross the beach; and the gapping teams were pinned down, with heavy losses. Subsequent waves of boats searched for gaps in vain, and were signaled off to land wherever they could. Such were the hazards of an amphibious assault, no matter how well equipped, trained, organized and planned.

**The cost: low tide on Omaha Beach, on the early afternoon of June 6. More than one in three of the 1,450 men of the first assault wave were killed or wounded. No matter how vast the resources and how meticulous the planning, an opposed amphibious landing remains among the most hazardous of all military operations.**

# INDEX

Figures in **bold** refer to illustrations

1st Armored Division 19
1st Army 26
1st Engineer Special Brigade 17
1st Infantry Division 7, 18
1st Infantry Division (British) 56
1st Marine Brigade 7
1st Marine Division 8
1st Medical Battalion 19
2nd Armored Division 8, 19
2nd Marine Division 8
2nd Ranger Battalion **22**
3rd Armored Division 19
3rd Infantry Division 8, **54**, 56
5th Army 56
7th Army 26
8th Amphibious Force 11, 56
8th Army (British) 56
9th Infantry Division 8
11th Amphibious Force 11
12th Amphibious Force 14, 15
25th Naval Construction Regiment 14
29th Infantry Division 19, 20
79th Armoured Division (British) 25
116th Regimental Combat Team 20
I Corps (Provisional) Atlantic Fleet 7

amphibious command ships (AGC) 31
Amphibious Corps, Atlantic Fleet 8
amphibious operations 5, 7, **H**(40), 47–59, 63
    codenames 11
    command and control 44–7
    fire support areas 46
    joint Army-Marine units 6–8
    landing sites **6, 16, 27, 46, 47, 48, 50, 52, 54,** 55
    logistics 27, 27–9, **28,** 29
    at night 5
    night retirement areas 46
    planning 9–11
        (1940–41) 6–8
    tactical development 5–11, 26, 44–7
    time designations (D-Day/H-Hour) 47–8
    variety of 4
amphibious vehicles, testing of 9
    *see also* Landing Craft; Landing Ships
antiaircraft artillery 18, **50**
*Anvil,* Operation 57
Anzio amphibious assault **52, 54,** 55–6
artificial harbors 15, **58**
Atlantic Amphibious Force 7
'Atlantic Wall' *see* German coastal defenses
Attack Cargo Ships (AKA) 30, 31
Attack Personnel Ships (APA) 30, 31
*Augusta*, USS **45,** 49
*Avalanche,* USS 54

barrage balloons 8, **16,** 27, **27,** 47
Battalion Landing Teams (BLT) 20–1
bazookas 22, **22**
Beach Jumper Units 16
beach landings *see* amphibious operations
beaches
    operational naming and numbering of 46–7
beachheads *see* amphibious operations: landing sites
Boat Teams 20–1, 22–3, **B**(34), 60–1
British forces 6, 25–7, 44, 54, 56, 57
    Landing Craft Assault (LCA) 22, **A5**(33), 41, 60
Browning Automatic Rifles (BAR) 22, **22**

Churchill Tanks and Armoured Vehicles 26
communications 29–30
Cunningham, Adm Sir Andrew 48, 51
Curtis, LtCdr Curtis 12

Davisville, Advance Proving Ground **43**
deception plans 10, 16
demolition and obstacle clearance 15–16, 25–7,
    **D**(36), 58, 61
destroyers **29**
Dieppe landings 9
doctrine of amphibious operations *see* amphibious
    operations: tactical development
*Dragoon,* Operation 57
DUKW amphibious truck **16, 23,** 25, 26, 46
Duplex Drive (DD) tanks 25, 26, **E**(37), **61,** 62
    *see also* Sherman M4 tank

Eisenhower, Gen Dwight 48, 54, 55–6
Emergency Striking Force 7
EMTO *see* European and Mediterranean Theater
    (EMTO)
Engineer Amphibian Command (EAC) 17
Engineer Special Brigades (ESB) 17
European and Mediterranean Theater (EMTO)
    extent of 3–4
    Pacific comparisons 3, 4, 9–10

*Fleet Training Publication No.167* 5

German coastal defenses 4, 9
Gustav Line 55

Harris Class transports 30
Hewitt, VAdm H. Kent 49, 51, 57
Higgins, Andrew 32, 41
howitzers
    ammunition **28**
    M7B1 105mm **21**
*Hunter Liggett,* USS **30**
*Husky,* Operation *see* Sicily amphibious assault

jeeps **7, 8**
Joint Assault Signal Company (JASCO) 30

Landing Craft 30–2, 41–4
    Assault (LCA) (British) 22, **A5**(33), 41, 60
    Assault Boat Teams 20–1, 22–3, **B**(34), 60–1
    Control (LCC) 44
    Infantry (LCI) 17, **A10**(33), **A11**(33), **C**(35), 42, **42, 43,** 54, 60, 61
    Gun (LCI (G)) 43
    Rocket (LCI (R)) 43
    lines of departure 46–7
    Mechanized (LCM) **14,** 17, 26, **A6**(33), **A7**(33), **F**(38), 41, **42,** 50, **57,** 60, 62
    Personnel (LCP) 32, **A1**(33), 33A2(33), 41, 50, 60
    Support (LCS) **43**
    Tank (LCT) **31, A8**(33), **A9**(33), 41, **41,** 44, **48,** 60
    Rocket (LCT(R)) **32, 43**
    Vehicle (LCV) **A3**(33), 60
    Vehicle or Personnel (LCVP) **7, 12,** 17, **18, 19, 20, 22, 22, A4**(33), **45,** 50, 60
landing forces 18–30
Landing Ship(s) 30–2, 31, 41–4
    assault assembly areas 46
    Infantry (LSI) **43**
    Mechanized (LSM) **43**
    Rocket (LSM(R)) 43
    Tank (LST) 4, **8,** 9, 10, **14,** 17, **27,** 41, **41,** 42, 44, **44, 50,**
Landing Vehicle
    Personnel (LVP) 22, **60**
    Tracked (LVT) (AMTRAC) 24
Lowry, RAdm Frank 56

machine guns **12, 22, 57**
mine detection **15, 60**
Monte Cassino, Battle of 56

mortars 22
Mulberry Artificial Harbours 15

Normandy amphibious assaults **3,** 17, 46, 59
North Africa amphibious assaults 6, 7, 9, 25, 48–51

obstacle clearance and demolition 15–16, 25–7,
    **D**(36), 58, 61
Omaha Beach 15, 20, **46, 47, 62, 63**
*Overlord,* Operation *see* Normandy amphibious assaults

Pacific theater 4, 5
    amphibious operations 3, 4, 9–10
paratroops 7, 9, 23
Patton, MajGen George 8, 49
pontoons **10, 14,** 15, 43, **43, 50**
    *see also* trackways

Ranger Battalions 23
recovery vehicles **25**
Regimental Combat Teams (RCT) 20–1
Rhino ferries and tugs 15, 43
Royal Navy 6

Salerno amphibious assault 53–5
Seabees *see* US Navy: Naval Construction Battalions
Sherman M4 tank 9, **24,** 25, **25, 26, E**(37), **F**(38), **48, 61,** 62
    *see also* Duplex Drive (DD) tanks
*Shingle,* Operation *see* Anzio amphibious assault
shore parties 27–9
Sicily amphibious assaults **50,** 51–3
signals 29–30
Smith, MajGen Holland 29
Sommerfield trackway **7,** 63
Stuart M5 tank 25

Task Force, Western Naval 58–9
Task Force 34 Western Naval Task Force, Morocco 49
Task Force 80 Western Naval Task Force 52
Task Force 81 56
    Gela Attack Force 'Dime' 53
    Southern Attack Force 54–5
Task Force 85 Scoglitti Attack Group 'Cent' 53
Task Force 86 Licata Attack Force 'Joss' 52
Task Force 87 53
*Tentative Manual for Landing Operations* 5
*Thompson,* USS **29**
*Torch,* Operation *see* North Africa amphibious assaults
trackways **G**(39), 63 *see also* pontoons
    Sommerfield **7,** 63
training 23–4
transport ships **30,** 30–2, 41–4
trucks
    2.5 ton 44
    DUKW amphibious **16, 23,** 25, 26, 46

US Army 5–6, 7, 8
US Fleet Marine Force 5
US Marine Corps 5–6, 7, 8
US Navy 6, 8, 9, 11–16, **12, 13**
    Beach Battalions 15
    Combat Demolition Units (NCDU) 15–16, 25–7,
        **D**(36), 58, 61
    communications 12
    Construction Battalion Maintenance Units and
        Detachments (CBMU) and (NCBD) 14
    Construction Battalions (NCB) **10, 13,** 13–15
    seaward areas 45–6
    unit numbering 12–13
Utah Beach 15, 17, 62

Weasel cargo carrier 25
Western Naval Task Force 58–9